I0721057

Queer ABC: A Small Dictionary of Queer Culture
Interpreted by: Riva Zmajoki
ARHO Press: Small Prints
By: Amazon KDP
Zagreb, October 2021
© Riva Zmajoki

Queer ABC

By Riva Zmajoki

Small Prints

Reader's Queer Passport:

(If you don't know how to fill it, read the book and fill the blank spaces as you understand the terms required of you to identify yourself.)

Name:

Birth Year:

Country of Origin:

Gender:

Gender Identity:

Gender Expression:

Social Gender:

Sex:

Sexual Orientation:

Romantic Inclination:

Given name:

Married name:

Pronoun:

Questioning phase:

Occupation:

Degree:

Other:

Level of Queerness:

Sections:

Introduction

We all start as embryos, therefore a neutral speck of tissue without gender, identity or sexuality, without religious afflictions or political stances.

As we grow in the womb, some of us transition from a neutral speck of tissue to a female, some to male, and some got confused and stay somewhere in the middle with their reproduction features mixed up.

The same gonads and tubes are used in both men, women and intersex people to create the complicated reproduction system that allows us to persist on into the future as a species that still didn't die out.

Nature, or Divine Being if you will, created us in such a way that reproduction activates, even if they often lead to great pain and sometimes even death, give us pleasure so we would be more inclined to engage in the activities that prolong lasting of our species on Earth.

I know you might find it discouraging that I'm connecting sexuality to reproduction repeatedly at the beginning of this journey but bear with me for a bit longer.

Before humans came in the state of a cultured being, sexuality was just a subset of reproduction. Our culture and our ability to comprehend and understand the world around us, as the world within us, allowed us to notice what pleasurable is and divide it from pain. We found a way to get pleasure while protecting ourselves against fertility which would burden us with constant childbearing and shorten our life spans.

That division brought on choices and choices led to differentiation.

People were now able to choose their sexual partners or refuse them altogether. They were able to spot when they like someone and when someone disgusts them enough to avoid being hit by a bat and dragged in the proverbial cave to mate for life.

That's how queer identities came to a life of struggling to find recognition, trying to establish a language which will make them accessible and visible to the rest of the breeding humanity. A language that will justify their stepping away from our duty as beings made for reproduction purposes.

Since we're cultured beings, our sole purpose isn't reproduction anymore. We have other things to offer to the whole that justify our existence in the collective.

There's work that gives us value, personal connections, creations, thoughts, the joy of sharing and simply existing as a unique individual.

Still, our sexual orientation and reproduction status are continuing to be things that interest our greater community and there is a need for us to justify and explain our existence before the world. To show what it is that makes us unique and worthy of love and light that were bestowed upon us by our birth.

To diminish the anxiety of that process and to prevent ourselves from being advocates constantly defending and explaining different variants of being queer, I created this small book that might come in handy.

I know, I know, this is the internet era, everything contained in here can be found somewhere online (except my own thoughts that will shade this piece of shattered glass through which you can look upon a world and see it anew) but bear in mind that our main questioning people (not those questioning themselves, they are quite sure who they are and where they stand, they are questioning us and our choices in life evaluating their worth) don't like to use the internet and google things. Even I, who isn't that old yet, often times forget I can google things I can't remember on the spot.

For those people on the fence, who still aren't straight out ballistic and hostile, you can borrow, or gift, them this book.

It will save you the effort, and often embarrassment, of explaining something shameful to your elder you have a great sense of respect towards.

On top of that, they will be able to decide what to search for and what to ignore. Maybe, who knows, they linger on and discover a thing or two more than you would explain to them yourself.

In this book, I tried to maintain a neutral stance so don't get all riled up when I describe and explain opposing points of view. In the end, there will be some reflections on the matter that are my own but I will point out that we went into the territory of speculation.

As a philosopher, a sociologist, a queer person and a writer, I feel competent enough to take this role on myself.

Hopefully,

I won't disappoint you beyond measure.

Riva Zmajoki

Issue One: Identity

To understand Queer Culture at all one must understand that it's never just about sexuality, it's primarily about identity and the right to maintain one.

As humans, we participate in many different circles playing many different roles. None of them is as important and impacting as the role of an intimate, sexual and/or emotional partner to another human being.

In order to be able to form such a relationship (or to refuse to play along and connect in any matter) we need to know our identity and what it entails because identity is the thing that will dictate how we behave and what we demand of others.

More often than not, we're not even aware of our identity, when the identity we have aligns perfectly with surrounding expectations of our behaviours. If that occurs, congratulations, you were born into the right gender and your sexual inclinations are socially acceptable enough for you never to be obligated to discuss them with anyone. Your gender expression is of the kind that doesn't create any discomfort wherever you go.

As such an individual, you have no need to explore your identity to details of scrutiny. You might find yourself annoyed or confused by the mere existence of a book like this one.

Still, since you're here, look around. You might find it as a useful tool for navigating the delicate nature of the expanding universe of queer meanings.

We become aware of the delicate nature of our identity when that identity clashes in any way with our surroundings. When what we put out for the world to see encounters with disgruntled disapproval or even hostility.

When identity becomes an obstacle which the group around us can't crack, the need for a specific and precise language arises.

As in any case of clashing cultures, language is of the utmost importance. It's a bridge that can explain frightening and foreign things to us. It can serve to present ourselves in the shortest possible terms.

In the story of the Babylon Tower, we can see how nothing can be built without understanding one another.

That's why we'll enter into this venture together, to make the navigation easier.

I'm aware that the language is hard enough as it is and incorporating new ways of expressing oneself and addressing others is exhausting but bear with me.

Language isn't a static thing. It's a moving matter that will escape and become something new in a heartbeat.

For now, to understand each other better we'll use these words to express understanding and convey support.

After all, prying into someone's sexuality is indecent in any era. It's better to educate yourself in the privacy of lines on the page. That way, if you get it wrong you can always direct them in my direction and say that I just taught you wrong.

Identity is usually a thing that consists of our different traits and abilities, of our roles and family relations. We can be a daughter that is lazy and stubborn. That can be the base of someone's identity.

For people who are born out of alignment with the surrounding norm for sexuality and gender, their sexuality and gender become the more important signifier of their identity than some other traits.

Here, we'll take a peek at some terms that those identities use to be able to talk and to understand what we're being told without needing an extensive explanation no one has time for. Not to listen to a speech or to deliver a skilled explanation.

Examples:

To define someone's Queer identity there are different things to take into account. Identity, Expression, Sexuality, Attraction, and Romanticism won't always align.

Usually, people only point out the parts of their identity that makes them queer but, in theory, any individual can have their own label of sexuality, even if it's the most common one like:

Straight, Male, MAAB, Heterosexual, Heteroromantic, Monosexual, Libidoist, Asian, Chinese

(I used Asian since it is the largest population on Earth, and Chinese because it's the largest ethnicity on Earth, also a man because by the latest count men are in the slight lead before women, only by a small percentage since men and women are about equally distributed in the population.)

The other example might be:

Lesbian, Female, MAAB, Trans Woman, Venusian, Polyamorous, African, Congolese

Or:

Fluid Gender, FAAB, Pansexual, European, Undocuqueer

More like it:

Non-Binary, Intersex, Sapiosexual, QTPOC, Male Presenting, Autist, Mix-Heritage, Brasilian

Female, FAAB, Asexual, Non-Libidoist, Deaf, POC, USA Citizen

Intersectionality is a theory that includes various signifiers of identity to establish someone's personal struggle and challenges before the adversity the world presents before them like racism, ableism, sexism, transphobia, homophobia and other ways humans create ideas to preserve their own sense of an inner circle that justifies keeping privilege in place.

Issue Two: Sexuality

Sexual attraction, or the lack of it, indicates who we like and who we dislike.

It's a question of who we want to engage with on a physical level.

We could make a table of possibilities, or more likely, I will do just that, make a table of possible connections and attractions. It's easier to navigate when you have a useful table than to visualise it all in your head. Thank me later.

In this time and age, it's most common for the attraction we experience to be the attraction of the opposite. That was easy when we thought of gender to be just two opposing parties. When gender gets blurred, the attraction gets a bit more diverse but don't worry it's still within basic arithmetic.

Still, when there is more than one option (that being one man/one woman option) it's advisable to have names so we don't have to go into details of description whenever we meet a new variant of things.

Keep in mind, those romantic feelings are here separated from sexual attraction because some people don't feel the same way as they desire.

Since feelings are more fleeting than physical reactions we'll limit ourselves on categorising sexuality, not romantic involvement.

You are> Attracted to ↓	Male Trans-Man	Female Trans-Woman	Non-Binary	Fluid Pan Agender…
Men	Gay	Straight	Androsexual	Androsexual
Trans-Men	Gay/ Skoliosexual	Straight/ Skoliosexual	Androsexual Skoliosexual	Androsexual Skoliosexual
Women	Straight	Lesbian	Gynesexual	Gynesexual
Trans-Women	Straight/ Skoliosexual	Lesbian/ Skoliosexual	Gynesexual/ Skoliosexual	Gynesexual/ Skoliosexual
Both Men and Women	Bisexual	Bisexual	Bisexual	Bisexual
Non-Binary	Bisexual/ Pansexual Skoliosexual	Bisexual/ Pansexual Skoliosexual	Bisexual/ Pansexual/ Skoliosexual	Bisexual/ Pansexual/ Skoliosexual
Fluid	Skoliosexual	Skoliosexual	Skoliosexual	Skoliosexual
No one	Asexual	Asexual	Asexual	Asexual
All Above	Pansexual/ Omnisexual Multisexual	Pansexual/ Omnisexual Multisexual	Pansexual/ Omnisexual Multisexual	Pansexual/ Omnisexual Multisexual
To Yourself	Autosexual	Autosexual	Autosexual	Autosexual
To More People at once	Polysexual	Polysexual	Polysexual	Polysexual
Don't want to label yourself	Pomosexual	Pomosexual	Pomosexual	Pomosexual
Intellect	Sapiosexual	Sapiosexual	Sapiosexual	Sapiosexual
Not Sure	Questioning	Questioning	Questioning	Questioning

So… it turned out that the table isn't so small but the terms are repeating themselves so it shouldn't be such a problem to memorise.

To any gender expressions which I didn't mention, I apologize but the page is wide only so much.

To march on, we'll shortly discuss gender and what it entails.

Issue Three: Gender

With gender, we enter the minefield that is the present-day discussion about gender and what it should be.

To navigate these stormy seas we'll keep in mind a few different layers of this discussion.

1. Gender expression is a way we show our gender on the outside, towards the world.

2. Gender identity is our inner sense of self (sometimes obscured from view out of the desire for safety, or privacy).

3. Gender roles are what society says gender should be.

4. Sex is the set-up of our genitalia. Genitalia set-up can be as we were born with or it can be surgically rearranged. (The main discussion that is lead these days is about how sex should, or shouldn't, determine our gender.)

5. Official Gender, or what our documents say we are.

6. Pronouns, or with what pronoun we are to be addressed by. (The discussion about pronouns struggles to determine the relation between Official Gender that should be put in our papers and Authentic Gender that is felt from within.)

There are many opposing views calling each other names and standing their ground. It's not just Pros and Cons but also insiders with a different view of things.

On one hand, we have feminists who think women (that are pronounced women at birth) should get protection from the ongoing inclusion of Trans Women into female spaces. The word they are known by is TERF.

On the other hand, some medically transitioned Trans People think there should be a difference between Trans People who medically transitioned and those who won't. They are called Transmedicalists.

Then there are people who simply fear Trans related issues and are a priori against it. Those are Transphobes.

Of course, some simply hate Trans People. You can think of them as Transmysogynists.

Also, there are those who think biology is the ultimate judge of what one's gender should be. You can call them Bioessentialists.

Those who support Trans Rights go by the name of People or Allies. (Just by that you can see where the discussion is going.)

Now, even among supporters, you have different streams of convictions.

Some people claim Gender is pretty much real. It's a fact. We are born male, female, or in the middle. This isn't related to biological sex but an identity that is within. For that kind of opinion, it's crucial and life-saving to allow the transition to anyone who needs it. It's a medical, scientific fact that can be objectively observed and measured.

On the opposite side, (even if it doesn't seem so) there are people who claim Gender is a social construct that has to be deconstructed. Gender is something that is a product of an oppressive system and we have to replace it with something new, something better.

It's ironic that in both parties, 'Gender is Real' and 'Gender is a Social Construct', there are people who oppose and people who support Trans Rights.

The argument is different for each and the argument can be pretty heated. As with any argument, all parties soon start to accuse the other side of trespassing and then they stop listening altogether.

In the midst of it, there are few topics that need to be resolved. It might seem trivial but sometimes those questions are the matter of life and death for those affected by those rules.

Just to have some insight we'll list a few of the problems.

1. Which bathrooms should Trans People go to? The ones that are in accordance with their Birth Sex, or the ones in accordance with their Gender Expression. (I say Gender Expression since it would be a serious intrusion of privacy if we asked for people to show us their genitalia before using the bathroom. This isn't an overstated fear, it's a thing that happens to people in airports.)

2. How should we address Trans People? How should we even ask them? (I know this is a sensitive issue especially since people who agree with their assigned gender get really offended when you miss-gender them. Further, a Trans Person can also get deeply offended for pointing out their struggle with expression.)

3. How curious can you be? (It's rude to ask about genitalia. Anything about genitalia is just rude anywhere. If you want to find out more, you can use google as well as this book. As you get friendlier with someone, the amount of details you get is up to you and your friend.)

4. Should children transition? (A question many spears have broken on.)

5. How early is too early for transition?

6. What about detransitioning?

7. What are the long-term consequences of transitioning?

8. How can one be sure they are Trans?

9. Trans Athletes, with whom they should compete?

10. How to talk with your children about this delicate topic?

For now, I'm not offering any answers. I'm just putting questions out there. Think about them and then listen to other people think. The future is what we make it to be. The world can be made a really miserable place but it also can be an experience to get joy from.

Since the ball is already rolling, there is no way to stop it. When an option is presented, it's nearly impossible to take it away. Still, the question is how far we're willing to go and what form of protection we'll offer to those boarding this new and uncertain train.

We should add a few more distinctions to navigate through terms with more ease.

1. Gender is binary (or, gender consists of two, not more not less, different categories, and all humans should fit either to one or the other.)

– Surprisingly, this stance doesn't exclude Trans People or transition. It aligns just fine with the transition as long as you choose which side of the binary you're standing on. It excludes all types of Non-Binary and Fluid people.

   –This stance goes well with 'Gender is Real' convictions, although it contradicts Bioessentialism since there are always people born with both variants of sex traits (see: Intersex).

   2. Gender is a spectrum (or, two opposing genders are not defined and closed. They are dots on the opposing sides of a spectrum, which means each of us consists of a different amount of characteristics that belong to either gender.)

   – On one hand this stance encourages any identity that is in the middle, or its lines are blurred. On the other hand, it makes it harder to determine with surety that someone is on the wrong side of the spectrum and should transition.

   – This stance goes well with the belief that Gender is a Social Construct.

ABC

+ *plus*

It's an addition to the LGBTQ acronym. It states that there are more sexualities and orientations that aren't included in the acronym but are still acknowledged as valid and included in the term.

Ableism

A prejudice that causes discrimination against disabled people.

Not defining the type of disability of the person, just stating that able people are more valuable than those who have disabilities of any kind.

Ace

A short way to say someone is Asexual in their sexual orientation.

Aceflux

A person whose sexual and romantic attractions change over time.

Acespike

An asexual person who usually doesn t experience sexual desire but sometimes has spikes of attraction.

Acevague

An asexual individual whose asexuality is caused by their neurodivergent mind. (Notice how the term doesn't state the type of asexuality the person in question is experiencing but rather the cause of said asexuality.)

Achillean

A man, or man-aligned person attracted to men. Also known as Men Loving Men.

Advocate

Someone who is actively fighting for the rights of sexual minorities.

Aegosexual

A person on the Asexual Spectrum who can feel sexual arousal but that arousal doesn't lead to feeling attraction, or a desire to engage with another person. (Also known as autochorisexual)

AFAB

Assigned Female at Birth

Agender

It refers to a person who feels the lack of gender thus has no desire to state which gender they belong to.

AIDS

Acquired Immunodeficiency Syndrome caused by HIV (human immunodeficiency virus).

Nowadays there are efficient treatments for the disease but it was incurable in the beginning. Since it was associated with the Gay community, it brought a great sense of stigma to Gay Men.

The controversy surrounding it is that it wasn't treated as a serious epidemic because it was widely spread in the queer community.

Allo

A short term for someone who experiences physical attraction. In opposition to the term of Ace and Aro.

Ally

A person who is not a part of the LGBT+ community but is supportive of it.

AMAB

Assigned Male at Birth

Androgynous

A person who display both male and female physical traits.

Androphobia

Intense fear of men.

Androsexual

A person who is attracted exclusively to men. That can include Gay Men, Straight women and everyone else who is strictly attracted to men.

Apothisexual

A person who is repulsed or disgusted by sexuality. (See also: Sex Repulsed.)

Aro

A short term standing for Aromantic Person.

Aromantic

A person who doesn't experience romantic feelings, or desires a romantic connection of any kind.

Asexual

A person who doesn't experience sexual attraction to anyone, or anything. The lack of attraction can be on the spectrum varying and changing. Their lack of attraction can be temporary as it can be a permanent state. (see also: Demisexual, Graysexual)

Asexual Spectrum

An umbrella term that encompasses various ways in which one's sexual orientation can express itself. It includes people who feel no to little sexual attraction that manifests itself under different sets of circumstances.

Asexual People may experience romantic affection.

Assigned Gender

A gender that is given to us by others. Usually at birth.

Assigned Pronoun

The way official documents and official languages describe us and words they want to address us with.

Assigned Sex

An estimation made by doctors upon birth by looking at our genitalia.

Assumed Gender

An estimation made by observers rooted in the way we look, or/and are expressing ourselves through clothes.

Attraction

An act, feeling or property of attraction.
An ability to attract something our way.

A sensation of being magnetically pulled towards something or someone that provokes desire within us.

The process of being drawn in towards someone or something.

Autoromantic

A person who has romantic feelings for oneself.

Autosexual

A person who experiences sexual attraction for oneself.

B

BDSM

An acronym that stands for Bondage Discipline (Dominance) Submission (Sadism) Masochism. It's a sexual practice that involves role-playing of dominance and often usage of whips, bondage and leather. It's a role-play, not real slavery. It can be practiced by people of different sexual orientations.

Bear

A gay man with a sturdy built and body hair.

Bellussexual

A person interested in certain aspects of sexuality, the aesthetic of a relationship or aspects of it but still doesn't want a sexual relationship (See also: Asexuality Spectrum)

Bi

A short term indicating that someone is Bisexual.

Bigenderflux

A person experiencing the bi-gender identity that fluctuates in intensity over time.

Bi-Curious

A way to say someone is considering if they are Bisexual or not.

Bi-Gender

Someone experiencing the state of having two genders at once.

Binder

An undergarment made for concealing breasts from being noticed.

Binding

A practice of concealing breasts. It's usually practised by Trans Men before Top Surgery while they are expressing their gender.

Bioessentialism

A stance that gender is determined by our biological sex. Usually, it's connected to our sex characteristics as well as X and Y chromosomes.

Biological Sex

It's the set of our genitalia as we were born with them. Also, it considers the number of X and Y chromosomes.

Biphobia

A fear of Bisexual people which leads to having a prejudice towards Bisexual People.

Bisexual

A person who is attracted to more than one gender. Usually, it's used for someone attracted both to men and women but it can also include other gender variants.

Blood Donation

A process of donating one's blood for medical purposes of saving lives. The process is voluntary and is considered an act of kindness.

Blood Donation Ban

Many countries have bans on gay and bisexual men giving blood donations. The ban can be permanent or it can demand from men engaging in sexual activities with other men to refrain from sexual intercourse for several months before being allowed to donate blood.

The controversial practice started in the midst of the AIDS pandemic when it still wasn't clear how it was transmitted and what caused it.

Boi

A black gay man. Used within the group of queer men of colour, not by outsiders.

Bottom

A gay man who prefers to be penetrated in sexual intercourse.

Bottom Surgery

A series of surgeries of genitalia Trans People go through to adjust their genitalia to their gender.

Butch

A masculine presenting lesbian.

C

48

Caedsexual

A person who was able to feel sexual attraction (was allo before) but lost it due to past trauma. (Asexuality Spectrum. Notice that it doesn't state the way the asexuality is expressed but rather what caused it.)

Celestial System

A subcategory of Xenogender in which people are partly, not completely, identifying with certain celestial bodies using their names to signify their sense of gender identity.

This system still uses terms such as feminine and masculine. There are about nineteen different ways to identify yourself in this system, as much as I'm aware of.

(Some identities mentioned in this dictionary are: Venusian, Neptunian, Saturnian and such. They shouldn't be confused with different terms using the same planets as a reference like Venusic, Neptunic etc. Similar, but not the same, is the Galactian Alignments way of viewing gender.)

Chosen Family

It's a group of people who give emotional and material support to an LGBT+ person. It's common because many queer-identifying people lose their families because of their identity.

CIS Gender

A person whose sex assigned at birth aligns with their gender. CIS is not an acronym, it's a Latin prefix that means *on this side of*.

Cisnormativity

An expectation that people around us have a gender that matches their sex assigned at birth.

Cissexism

A belief that Trans People are inferior to Cispeople.

Closeted

A person that doesn't want others to know they are LGBT+.

Co

One of the suggested neutral pronouns in the third gender that avoids mentioning or assuming someone's gender. It's meant to be used for non-binary individuals.

Nominative   Co
Accusative Co

Pronominal Possessive　　　Cos/Co's

Predicative Possessive　　　Co's

Reflexive　　Coself

Coming Out

A person who is ready to publicly tell what their sexual orientation/gender/identity is. The term refers to coming out of the closet. Closet being the proverbial denial and secrecy.

Conforming

A state of agreeing to play along with social norms and rules of engagement.

Crossdressing

An act of dressing in the clothes of the gender you don't belong to.

Culturally Queer

People who are raised by queer parents, or are socializing with queer people so much that they think of themselves as belonging to the queer culture even if they themselves aren't queer.

Culture

A term that encompasses the way social groups gain and maintain their common identity by practising similar values, habits, traits, expressions, and beliefs.

It also may refer to any sociological, philosophical, religious or ethnic construct produced by human action. (Example: When visiting a foreign country, you admire its rich culture by observing its buildings and noticing the behaviours of native citizens.)

Cupiosexual

A person who doesn't experience sexual attraction but still desires to engage in a sexual relationship, or sexual behaviour. It's a subset of the Asexual Spectrum.

D

54

Deadnaming

Calling a Trans Person by their given name they aren't using anymore. They consider their given name to be dead.

Demiboy

A person that is partly male. They identify with the male gender but not completely. Sometimes they also identify as partly Agender. This doesn't relate to their Assigned Sex at all.

Demigirl

A person that is partly female. They identify with the female gender but not completely. They can partly identify as Agender or other identities. This doesn't relate to their Assigned Sex.

Demiromantic

A person who experiences romantic feelings only after a strong emotional bond is formed. It's a subset of the Aromantic Spectrum.

Demisexual

A person who experiences sexual attraction only after a strong emotional bond is formed. It's a subset of an Asexual Spectrum.

Detransitioning

A process of reversing the transitioning process. When a person decides to return to their Assigned Gender, be it permanent or temporary.

Deviation

Something that departs, distinguishes itself or varies from the standard, or the expected value.

In queerness, you might say that any kind of queerness was viewed as deviation at some point in history in different parts of the world, and somewhere are still viewed like that to this day.

The process of normalization of queerness and gaining rights and protections by the state is the process of diminishing the sense of deviation when we encounter a queer person.

Disclosure

When someone exposes somebody's Trans Identity without consent or approval of the Trans Person in question.

Discrimination

An act of differentiating between different values. In human interaction:

An act of treating various humans differently based on their perceived gender, race, sexuality, religion, ethnicity and other traits like them. Mostly, it's referred to as treating people unjustly, cruelly and taking away opportunities based on the trait, or based on the group someone considers to be less worthy, or valuable.

Disgust

Feeling repulsion and nausea by something unpleasant and potentially poisonous.

Divinity

A being, or a set of beings, believed to exist beyond the visible material realm possessing powers that go above and beyond usual material limitations like laws of physics.

Down Low (DL)

An African-American slang for men who identify as heterosexual but engage in sex with men.

Drag Queens/Kings

People dressing up fabulously into robes of the gender they don't belong to.

Dyke

Once a derogatory term for a lesbian. Lately, reclaimed by some circles of lesbians.

E

Emotions

An inner mechanism of the biological release of different hormones causing affectionate states we interpret as emotions.

It's a way our mind interprets our bodily states as psychological states and responses.

Ethnicity

A group of people who identify as a coherent group based on their shared cultural identity, language, history, religion and similar signifiers caused by experience and culture.

It's a broader term than race because it doesn't focus on the physical characteristics of its members and can include members of various different races.

Evolution

The term comes from biology. It means that species change over several generations creating new improved versions of themselves that are better adapted to their environment.

The term is also used to describe similar processes in other areas of our experience.

Likewise, language is one of the human structures that is submittal to change and is always changing to include, or abandon, words that express the current state of human experience.

Experience

A process of gaining knowledge by interacting with the world around us.

A skill gained by practising.

Perceiving the world around us.

A thing that happened.

Knowledge gained through doing, living, observing the world around us.

Extremism

It's a set of beliefs that go to extremes. Views that further themselves from the mainstream worldview. It can be in religion, politics, or any other structure of beliefs.

People holding extreme beliefs have justifications inside of those belief structures that justify the, sometimes extreme, measures they are willing to take to prevent, or push, a certain agenda.

Take note that the end *–ism* is used in words like sexism, racism, ableism, etc. It's a way to describe that those beliefs are being abandoned by the mainstream belief structure.

The view on what is considered to be extreme is also submittal to change and re-evaluation by the broader society. In the past, queer theories were viewed as extremes that weren't acceptable and sexism along with racism were common practices that were considered normal and natural.

65

F

FAAB

Female Assigned at Birth

Fact

Something that exists in the world and can't be argued or disproved its existence.

Something that exists.

Something proved by observation and examination.

Fag

A slur for a gay man. Although it's reclaimed by some circles.

Fan-Fiction

A piece of fiction made by fans of an original authored piece of art. Usually, it's in written form but can also be made in visual media, and other forms of artistic expression as paintings, drawings and, but not limited to, altered pictures.

In queer culture, it's an act of inserting queerness in a piece of fiction we highly value. It's either to show the Queer Coded nature of the characters we observe and are frustrated by or just plainly making everyone gay for their own sense of identity and validation.

Femme

A lesbian, a female attracted to other females, with a feminine expression. (see also: Lipstick Lesbian)

Feminism

A movement that fights for women's rights. Once upon a time, it was a radical extremist movement where women chained themselves to railroads to get the right to vote and work.

Nowadays it's a discussion about privilege, inequality and disadvantages of minorities. The struggle to keep women safe and equal before the law and in everyday life is still real. Especially in the countries where human rights aren't fully established.

(Note: one can notice how the movement still carries its *–ism* ending that stated them as an extremist movement. See: Extremism.)

Fertility

An ability to conceive and birth a child. It's the most common argument against early transition because one of the side-effects of medical transition is infertility that oftentimes can't be reversed. It's a question of how much a child can understand about infertility to consent to lose it.

(I may say that it somehow seems understandable that feminists who are primarily concerned for the safety of female bodies and invested in removing reproduction restrictions are concerned about the fertility of young people.)

Fetish

A sexual desire, or attraction, caused by an inanimate object. Or an object of worshipping and desire. An attribution of inherent value to an object, be it in sexuality or devotion practices.

Fetishism

A process of displacing sexual desire, or devotion, to inanimate objects, or non-sexual parts of the anatomy. (Example: clothes, shoes, etc.)

Fictosexual

A person who experiences sexual desire towards fictional characters. Usually 2D characters. (It falls under the asexual umbrella subset of aegosexuality.)

Fingender

An umbrella term for any gender that has primary feminine qualities to it.

Flags

A way to express and identify your orientation and gender without talking about it.

Fluid

Refusal to firmly establish one's identity or orientation. It means that person experiences changes in their identity, orientation and inclinations.

Fraysexual

A person whose sense of sexual attraction diminishes and fades after getting to know someone. (Notice how this is opposite to the Demisexual Orientation. It's on the Asexual Spectrum.)

FTM

Female To Male. It marks the process of transition for Trans People.

G

Galactian Alignment System

A gender system for non-binary individuals who don't want to determine their gender by the standard duality of male and female qualities but rather use neutral genderless space objects.

In contrast to the Celestial System or the general Xenogender category, here the names of the space objects are used only as signifiers, an aesthetic name rather than identifying with objects themselves. The names are only an indication of gender but an individual can still identify into an object as a personal choice.

(The basic alignments are: Aurorian, Lunarian, Solarian, Stellarian, Spacialian, Singularian. The terms are further combined to create unique identities such as, but not limited to Eclipsian, Nebularian, Cometian, etc.)

Gatekeeping

When a member of a community decides who does and who doesn't belong to a certain circle of queer identities. It's considered harmful and not advisable.

Gauss Curve

A normal, or standard, distribution for independent randomly generated variables in a binominal distribution of events.

(Also: Gaussian Curvature, Gaussian Distribution, Bell Curve.)

Gay

A man who has an exclusive attraction to other men.

Gay Marriage

Also used: Marriage Equality. A stance that queer people too should have access to marriage and all its privileges.

Gaydar

A slang term for being able to spot who's gay, as in radar for spotting gays.

Gender

A set of social behaviours, rules of engagement and catalogue of clothes. One who's belonging to a certain gender must abide by.

Genderless

A person experiencing the lack of any gender identity whatsoever. (See also: Agender, Gendervoid.)

Gendervoid

A person whose identity doesn't connect to any gender in particular. (Also known as Agender and Genderless.)

Gender Affirming Surgery

Any set of surgeries a Transgender Person chooses to undergo to align their physical appearance to their inner gender identity.

Gender Bending

Challenging of what is acceptable for a certain gender to express or do.

Gender Binary

The stance that there are only and exclusively two genders, male and female.

Gender Dysphoria

A state of mental and physical discomfort an individual experiences when they have a sense that their identity doesn't match up with their physical body. It can vary in the intensity and stress it induces in people. Often, it's a medical indicator of an urgency with which someone is in a need of a medical transition.

Gender Euphoria

A state of euphoria caused by someone acknowledging the inner gender as valid.

Gender Expansive

A state of gender expression that exceeds the limitations of the given gender. (See also: Non-Binary)

Gender Expression

Outer signs of gender like clothes, make-up, behaviours, postures and all forms of expressing one's gender, which doesn't have to align with the inner sense of gender.

Gender Fluid

A state of experiencing your gender changing and not being fixed. Not staying the same all the time.

Gender Identity

The inner sense of one's own gender. It doesn't matter if that gender identity aligns with the common sense of identity, or if it defies common signifiers. Even if the identity is the lack of gender, that is gender identity in itself.

Gender is a Social Construct

The belief that gender is nothing but a social construct of randomly placed characteristics that have no physical connection to the biology of sex.

Gender is Real

The belief that our mind is inherently gendered and that there are measurable differences between men and women. If one who believes gender is real accepts the existence of more than two genders, they think that even those in between can be scientifically measured and categorised.

Gender Neutral Pronouns

Pronouns that don't assume gender. A way to address people without labelling their gender. Most commonly used pronouns are They/Them but there are many offered variants.

Gender Performance Theory

The theory that gender isn't inherently naturally embedded in us but learned through cultural practices. It states that we daily decide how we'll perform our gender socially based on our own interpretation of gender rules that are bestowed upon us by the society we live in.

Gender Roles

A set of rules that define and manage how differently gendered people should or shouldn't behave, dress, act, express themselves and feel.

Genderqueer

A person who doesn't follow established gender norms for binary gender expression and identity. It includes Agender, Non-Binary, Fluid, Pangender and other identities that don't follow binary logic.

Gillick Competence

A term that is used in medical law to determine if a child under 16 years of age has enough intelligence, competence and understanding to fully comprehend the medical treatment they are agreeing to take without their parents, or guardians, permission.

Googling

A process of searching information online, on servers connected through interconnected web of servers, using search engines created for the purpose of giving out specific data.

Google is a search engine that is most popular and commonly used for online searches. So much so, that the mere process of searching for data online is called by its name.

Gray-aromantic

A person who falls on the spectrum of romantic emotions somewhere between an Aromantic Person who doesn't experience romantic feelings and people who experience romantic feelings. (They experience it sometimes and under certain circumstances. See also: Demiromantic)

Gray-asexual

A person who falls on the spectrum of sexuality somewhere between an Asexual Person who doesn't experience sexual attraction and people who experience sexual attraction. (They experience it sometimes under certain circumstances. See also: Demisexual)

GSM

Gender and Sexual Minorities

Gynesexual

Or Gynosexual is a person attracted to femininity. This term is used regardless of what gender expression or identity the person experiencing this attraction has. It includes straight men, lesbians and every other category of people attracted to femininity. Femininity here isn't limited to set up of someone's genitalia.

H

82

He/Him

Pronouns signifying that someone's gender is male.

Hermaphrodite

An outdated term that was used to describe Intersex People. Nowadays it's considered to be an insult.

Heteroflexible

A person who primarily identifies as heterosexual but sometimes experiences homosexual attraction and engages in homosexual intercourse.

(The term is criticised for expressing internalized biphobia.)

Homoflexible

A person who primarily identifies as homosexual but sometimes experiences heterosexual attraction and engages in heterosexual intercourse.

(The term is criticised for expressing internalized biphobia.)

Homophobia

An irrational fear, or prejudice, against homosexual people.

It can be expressed through the individual expression of sentiment, aggressive actions, or through systemic discrimination implemented through laws and restrictions placed against homosexual individuals.

Homosexual

A term used to describe people attracted to members of their own sex. The term is nowadays considered to be offensive and the word gay is commonly used instead.

Hormones

A type of signalling molecule that relays messages between tissues and organs regulated by the brain. They are transported through blood, or sap, from organs that produce them to tissue that needs to execute a required action.

Sex hormones control primary and secondary sex characteristics.

Hormone Blockers

Or Puberty Blockers, are supplement hormones that block puberty from starting. It's intended to give the child who struggles with gender identity more time to decide and realize what their gender is, to reach an age where they can make an informed and mature decision about their further development.

Heteronormativity

A social assumption that the normal sexuality is heterosexuality, that gender is binary and that relationships and marital connections are between a man and a woman.

It's a belief that contains an undertone of morality and values. A base for discriminating against people who don't fit the moral assumed norm, who deviate from the standard.

Heterosexual

A person attracted to a gender opposite to their own.

Hyperfemininty

An overstate display of femininity that can be perceived as playing a stereotype.

When an individual practices the traditionally perceived feminine role to an over adherence of a stereotypical role of what a woman should be and how she should behave.

Hypermasculinity

A state of overstating traits that are socially perceived as typically masculine such as strength, aggression, virility, physicality, and sexuality.

Hysteria

An emotional state of excess emotions.
Once it was a medical diagnosis.

I

Iamvanosexual

A sexual orientation when someone enjoys having sexual acts performed on them but does not want to perform sexual acts on other people. They may be sex repulsed, or sex neutral when it comes to performing sexual acts. (Asexual Spectrum. See opposite: Placiosexual.)

In the Closet

An expression to say that someone isn't comfortable in sharing their queer sexuality or gender identity with others. Thus they are living in the closet and not openly.

Inclusive Language

A type of lingual expression that tries to avoid being offensive to minorities no matter the character of those minorities. It's an effort to avoid using words that imply that we're being sexist, racist, phobic, or offensive in any manner. An example of that can be using neutral pronouns and expressions that don't imply masculinity or assume gender.

Internalized Homophobia

A state of a queer person internalizing the prejudice towards their own queerness and believing in harmful stereotypes projecting them on other members of the queer community adding up to the validity of those same prejudices.

Intersectionality

It's a theory that explains how one's gender, social status, race, individual traits and political identities intersect to create a unique position of privilege and disadvantage. It states how everyone experiences an individual process of privilege and oppression.

This theory offers a framework to show how affected different social groups and different individuals are by their own set of prejudices they face and their own set of privileges they receive from their surrounding environment.

Intersex

A person who is born with natural variations where their genitals, gonads, hormones, chromosomes or reproductive organs don't fit the binary norm of belonging to either male or female sex. They have characteristics that can't be categorised into only one sex. This state is related to physical and sexual characteristics and has nothing to do with the inner sense of gender or sexual orientation. It's estimated that 1.7% of the population is born with intersex traits

(there are as many intersex people in the world as
there are redheads).

J

94

Jezebel

Stating that a woman is an immoral seductress. Based on a historical woman mentioned in the Bible who persecuted Jews because of their religion. She was described as cruel and merciless.

Justice

A sense of fairness and protection by the law. In queer culture, it's a long-standing fight to receive justice and equal standing with the surrounding mainly heterosexual cisgendered society.

It's an ideal that states how any systemic injustices can be rectified. A belief that moves us to try to end all discrimination minorities are experiencing in the world which opposes them.

K

Kafkaesque

Situations that are senseless, illogical, complex, surreal or nightmarish.

Based on the name of Franz Kafka (1883–1924) German-speaking Bohemian novelist and short story writer.

Kink

A sexual behaviour that falls out of the socially acceptable forms of sexual behaviour. Unconventional sexual preference. Not limited to the queer population. (See also: Fetish, a sub-set of Kink)

Kinsey Scale

A first scale that suggests how sexual orientation isn't binary but a spectrum that varies. It was set in 1948 by Alfred Kinsey. As you might guess by the year of its creation, some are challenging the limitation of the same scale and its ability to determine the diverse way we think of sexuality these days.

Also known as the Heterosexual-Homosexual Rating Scale.

Some of its limitations:

1. It doesn't make a distinction between romantic and sexual orientation.

2. It doesn't account for asexuality.

3. It assumes gender is binary.

4. It reduces bisexuality to a point between heterosexuality and homosexuality.

5. People feel discomfort when they are reduced to a number and that number can change as people's experiences change.

These days there are over 200 scales that are trying to find a suitable way to categorise and determine someone's sexual and romantic orientation.

L

102

Label

A piece of paper or plastic attached to an object describing it and stating its price.

When put on a person, a defining characteristic that diminishes a person to a said characteristic like Queer, Gay, black, woman, tall. Usually, it was considered a limiting and insulting practice especially when it's restrictive and/or inaccurate.

Queer labels, a way to reclaim identity and change the content of the label from insulting and derogatory to empowering and validating.

Label Free

The label that states the person in question doesn't want to attach themselves to any labels.

Latinx

The neutral way to address a Latino person without stating their gender.

Legal Transition

A term that refers to all the paperwork that is needed for someone's gender to be changed. It's a way to point out how costly and hard it is for a person to legally change their gender.

Legality

A state of being in accordance, or complying, comforting and agreeing, with the law. (Law being, usually, a written agreement between humans stating which rules should be obligatory by all participants of the society and which rules, when broken, demand for the punishment to be implemented.)

Lesbian

A female-gendered person attracted exclusively to female-gendered people.

Lesbos

A Greek Island on which Sappho (an Ancient Greek poet writing lesbian erotic poetry) was born.

Lesbophobia

A state of prejudice and fear before Lesbians

LGBT

Lesbian Gay Bisexual Transgender

LGBTQIA+

Lesbian Gay Bisexual Transgender Queer Intersex Asexual plus

LGBTQIAPD

Lesbian Gay Bisexual Transgender Queer Intersex Asexual Pansexual Demisexual

LGBTQIAPK

Lesbian Gay Bisexual Transgender Queer/Questioning Intersex Asexual Pansexual Kink

LGBTQQIAAP

Lesbian Gay Bisexual Transgender Queer Questioning Intersex Ally Asexual Pansexual

Libidoist Asexual

An asexual person who is rarely, or never attracted to other people but does experience sex drive, or has a libido that doesn't lead to sexual activities with other people.

Libidoist Sexual

A person who has both a libido and is attracted to other people.

Lifestyle

A term that is used to signify how a queer sexual orientation or gender identity is something that can be chosen like a lifestyle rather than something that is given like an orientation.

Lingender

An umbrella term for any gender that has primary androgynous qualities to it.

Lipstick Lesbian

A lesbian with a feminine gender expression.

Lithosexual

A person who does feel sexual attraction but doesn't want for that attraction to be reciprocated. (Formerly known as Akiosexual. Asexual Spectrum.)

Living Openly

A queer person living their life openly and sharing their queer identity without restrictions.

Lunarians

A non-binary person who is feminine aligned in expression or identity.

M

MAAB

Male Assigned at Birth

Man

A gender category that is defined through the rules and expression of masculinity. It usually entails traits like aggressiveness, assertiveness, sturdiness, short hair, short nails, trousers, overalls, a lack of jewellery, short heels, and other signifiers of outer expressing. Within biology, it's signified with the lack of ability to birth children, breastfeed and menstruate. Having a penis and testicles is also one of the tell signs of a male. Still, even if you spot all mentioned above, caution is advised. In this day and age, you never can tell for sure.

(Side note: I'm well aware that this definition alone can be rage-inducing but in the lack of other signifiers it's hard to determine a man without resorting to biology, or emotions. At least, I didn't succumb in listing things a man can or can not do.)

(Side-side note: This description is based on the current Western expression of the male gender role. We should be aware that in other parts of the globe men do wear dresses Snd jewellery, and high heels were a worn by men when they were invented.)

Marriage

A cultural recognition of a union between two individuals.

It varies from culture to culture but some aspects of it are usually regulated by law. It comes with certain obligations and duties, but it also provides certain rights, like the visitation of your spouse in the hospital, making decisions in the name of your spouse when they can't and sharing the material wealth.

Marriage Equality

A fight of queer people to gain access to the institution of marriage so they can gain the same protection and rights before the law as heterosexual couples do.

Masc

Masculine gender expression of a queer-identifying person.

Its controversy is of how it's used in gay dating culture to signify a preference and exclude any men that present, or are, feminine in any way.

Medical Transition

A process of changing one's gender through medical procedures that realign the set-up of one's genitalia/secondary sexual characteristics.

Metrosexual

A heterosexual man having a gender expression that is not fitting to the stereotypical male role.

Mingender

An umbrella term for any gender that has primary masculine qualities to it.

Misgendering

Calling a person a gender they don't feel they belong to.

Mispronoun

When you use the wrong pronoun to address the person in question.

MLM

Men Loving Men
Usually used by communities of colour to signify how the person in question prefers men to other

genders not stating the rest of that person's orientation.

Monogamous

Having a relationship only with one partner at a time.

Monolith

A single upright block of stone. Used to describe structures that are slow to change and not dividable.

In Queer Culture, the insistence that being queer isn't a monolithic structure but diverse and consistent of many different changing subsets of traits and values.

Monosexual

A person attracted to only one gender identity, expression, sex.

MSM

Men having sex with men

Its origin was in the wake of the AIDS pandemic to make a distinction between different sexual orientations and establish which men have sex with men because they were perceived as the main carriers of HIV. (It includes gay, bisexual, pansexual, heteroflexible, homoflexible and all other categories of men who ever have any sexual encounter with other men.)

It's criticised for erasing the identity of sexual minorities putting them all in the same level of risk for contracting AIDS.

MTF

Male Transitioning to Female

MTX

Male Transitioning to Genderqueer, or a gender expansive identity.

Multisexual

A person attracted to more than one gender identity, gender expression, sex or the combination of those.

Mx.

A neutral replacement for Ms. or Mr.

Myrsexual

A state of experiencing different asexual identities that are happening at the same time or exchanging, causing for the individual to be unable to put themselves under one label of Asexual Spectrum.

N

Neopronouns

Any set of third-person singular pronouns which are still not recognized and categorized by the official language they are used in. It's a measure which for some people expresses their gender more accurately than a neutral third person pronoun of their language.

It also may serve as a way to distinguish between singular for a non-binary person and a third person plural, or third person pronoun for a thing.

The critique some (sometimes Transmedicalists) have about neopronouns is that they promote ableism and are hard to use by people that aren't neuro-typical.

Some, but not all, suggested that neopronouns can be: Ae, Co, E, Ey, Fae, Hu, It, One, Per, Ve, Xe, Ze.

(See examples: Co, Thon, Ve, Xe, Ze)

Neptunic

Attraction towards women, feminine non-binary people and neutral non-binary people. The term is usually used by non-binary people that don't want to state their gender and want to say that they aren't attracted to masculinity in any form.

(Also called: Nomascsexual)

Nibling

A gender neutral way to address children of one's sibling. It can be used instead of niece, or nephew.

Nomasexual

Attraction to all gender identities except to binary men. (Notice how here the orientation is defined by repulsion, not attraction.)

Nominsexual

Attraction to all gender identities except to those that are masculine in nature, their gender or/and presentation. (Notice how here the difference is that all masculinity is excluded from attraction, not just binary men as in Nomasexual.)

Non-Binary Gender

A person whose gender identity doesn't fall into binary categories of gender or rather fall somewhere on the spectrum of the two as opposing points. Sometimes a person denounces gender altogether taking in agender identity.

Non-Conforming

A person who doesn't conform to common ways things are done. In a context of queerness, it's a person who refuses to play by gender rules described by society.

Non-Libidoist Asexual

It's an asexual person who doesn't experience any sex drive or libido.

Norm

Something that is usual, typical or standard.

A behaviour that is considered to be normal in a certain society.

Omnisexual

A person attracted to every, and any, gender identity, gender expression or the lack of it. (An example in Fiction: Captain Jack Harkness, Doctor Who.)

Openly Gay

A person who comfortably and gladly shares their LGBT+ identities with the world.

Orientation

A word that signifies that someone's sexual, or romantic, orientation isn't a choice but engraved within their psyche.

Out

A state of being out in the open. A person who is comfortable with sharing their queer identity with society.

Outing

An act of revealing someone's sexual or gender identity without their consent, or agreement.

P

126

Pangender

A person experiencing the state of having more than one sense of their own inner gender.

Panromantic

A person capable of experiencing romantic feelings for more than one gender identity, of gender expression.

Pansexual

A person attracted to more than one gender identity, or gender expression.

Partner or Significant Other

A neutral term for saying you have a romantic relationship with someone without stating gender or marrital status.

Passing

A term that signifies when a Trans Person can pass for a person born into the gender they are transitioning into.

PGP

Preferred gender pronouns

Philosophy

1. Love for wisdom.

2. A set of values one can lead their life by.

3. A study of values, nature, the nature of the divine, the nature of self, the meaning of life, the structure of nature, the structure of the universe, the structure of language, logic, morality, humanity, legality, sexuality, and other things (other things being everything and anything you can think of that is worth thinking about.)

Phobia

An extreme, or irrational fear of something.

Placiosexual

A sexual orientation when someone enjoys performing sexual acts but does not want for sexual acts to be performed on them. They may be sex repulsed, or sex neutral when it comes to sexual acts that could be performed on them. (Asexual Spectrum. See the opposite orientation: Iamvanosexual)

Positive

When a person is positive for AIDS.

Polyamory

People who have multiple love, intimate and emotional relationships at the same time.

Polysexual

People who have multiple sexual relationships at the same time.

Pomosexual

A person who rejects any kinds of labels connected through their sexuality or romantic attraction.

Post-Op

A way to say that a Trans Person had their surgeries to transition to their inner gender.

Pre-Op

A way to say that a Trans Person didn't go through sex affirming surgeries.

Preference

A way to say a person prefers something over something else. It signifies that there is a choice. It can be used for people with identities that have multiple choices but have preferences for one of those options.

Pride

A yearly celebration to mark the sense of pride for being queer.

Privilege

An exclusive right, advantage or opportunity granted to an individual by their status in a certain social group, by characteristics generally favoured by general society, or some other random trait the individual possesses.

Promiscuity

A Sexual Behaviour of frequent sexual activity with different partners, or a person who is indiscriminate in their choice of sexual partners.

Pronouns

A way to address people that signifies their gender.

PTP

People raised by a trans parent.

Q

QPOC

Queer People of Colour

Used to show how queer people of colour have their own unique challenges in addition to being queer that is caused by their skin tone.

QTPOC

Queer and Transgender People of Colour

Queer as a Slur

Once upon a time, this word was used as an insult and the hurt of it still aches some people. To those who feel discomfort before it, it's polite not to use it.

Queer as Identity

Queer is one of the words that went through evolution in the English language. Once it was used as a slur to offend people of different gender, expression, identity or orientation.

Lately, it's been reclaimed as a legitimate word to describe LGBTIAPDK+ identities in a simpler manner. Still, for its history, not all people are glad to hear it.

(Note: In this book, I've been using it interchangeably with the LGBT+ label because I feel comfortable with it. I do apologize to anyone who feels uncomfortable by it.)

Queer Coding

When a character in fiction is given stereotypically queer behaviours, voices, clothes, mannerisms and other traits but isn't explicitly shown, told or exposed as being queer.

It's a practice that started in the time when queer characters were a cause for a movie to be censored or banned. It was a way to include queer stories and characters without being banned from showing the movie to audiences.

It continues to this day but nowadays it's called Queerbaiting.

Queerbaiting

A practice used in entertainment and marketing to overstate queer presence in their product to attract a queer audience just to get a minimal representation, or sometimes even implied representation.

Queerspawn

People who were raised by one or more queer parents, guardians or caretakers.

Questioning

A process of discovering one's sexuality, gender, or orientation. It's a time of questioning one's identity.

Growing up in an environment that enforces heteronormative stereotypes can leave some people unsure of their own sexuality, identity or gender. Many queer people discover their sexuality in later stages of their life.

R

Race

A way to distinguish different human groups into separate categories by their physical traits like skin colour, eye shape, hair type and other traits.

It's a term that changes over time and is viewed differently in different cultures.

Some argue races are easily distinguishable and biologically imperative, others argue it's just a social construct without any inherent value.

Racism

A prejudice, discrimination or antagonism directed at other people who are viewed as a part of a certain racial or ethnic group. That group is usually viewed as a minority or is marginalized.

It's a belief about how race is something inherent in people that produces palpable and measurable differences between different races. This belief leads some people to believe how people should be divided into separate entities based on their race.

Rainbow

A symbol of Queer culture. The flag should encompass all the variants of queer identities, sexualities, genders and expressions.

Reciprosexual

A person who feels sexual attraction only after they know someone is already attracted to them. (It's on Asexual Spectrum.)

Religion

A set of beliefs in a specific sort of divinity that is a target of devotion and a source of protection. It includes practices, rituals, restrictions and rules.

Usually, it forms a social group that identify by their membership in a certain religion.

It's a source of pride, disputes, wars and arguments of all kinds since most of the religions are exclusive groups that claim to be in possession of privilege no one else can get access to but by joining their group.

Requissexual

A person who experiences little to no sexual attraction to others due to some state of emotional exhaustion.

Roman Mythology

A set of myths, beliefs and arts that were the base of the culture of Ancient Rome. Some of their myths were borrowed, or influenced, by Ancient Greeks and neighbouring nations but renamed and re-purposed.

Romantic Orientation

An identity that states if a person experience romantic feelings. If they do, it states in what way or form.

S

SAAB

Sex Assigned at Birth

Same Gender Loving (SGL)

People who are romantically attracted to the same gender as they are.

Sapiosexual

A person attracted to another person's personality and mind rather than their genitalia or gender.

Sapphic

Also known as Lesbians. The name derives from the name of the Ancient Greek poet Sappho.

Saturnic

Attraction to androgynous individuals and people who exhibition androgynous traits rather than binary gender identities. (Notice how this attraction doesn't reveal the gender of the person in question and is based on the repulsion of the binary identities.)

Self-Worth

A sense that there is inherent value to our person.

Sex

Set up of genitalia that determines gender.
Also, a sexual act between people.

Sex Averse

People who don't want to have sex and find the thought of it unappealing, disturbing, repulsive or disgusting. Also known as Sex Repulsed.
(On an Asexual Spectrum)

Sex Favourable

People who enjoy some aspects of sex even if they don't experience that kind of attraction. Also known as Sex Positive.
(On an Asexual Spectrum)

Sex Indifferent

People who don't feel any preference about sex. They don't experience any strong feelings towards sex. Also known as Sex Neutral.
(On an Asexual Spectrum)

Sexism

A prejudice, or discrimination, based on someone's sex or gender. Most commonly targeted at women. It can include the idea that one sex is intrinsically superior to others.

Sexual Behaviour

A broad spectrum of behaviours in which people engage with each other. Those behaviours connect to sexuality, reproduction and pleasure.

Sexual Minority

A group of people whose sexual orientation, identity, or behaviour differs from the majority that surrounds them.

Sexual Orientation

A consistent pattern of behaviours and attractions a person has towards other people based on their gender identity, gender expression, sex and other characteristics some might find simulative, attractive, or repulsive for that matter.

(Sometimes people define their orientation by the gender they aren't attracted to rather than to that they are.)

Sexualisation

To put sexual lenses in observing someone, or something, thinking of them primarily in a sexual context.

The extreme example of this is when a person is stopped being viewed as a person but rather as an object, a thing that has value in its sexual appeal rather than other characteristics of their personality.

Sexuality

The way people express themselves sexually. This involves erotic, romantic, biological, physical, emotional, spiritual, or social feelings and behaviours.

It's a broad term with no clear definition because it's ever-changing since societies change their stance on sexuality as the time passes.

She/Her

Pronouns that signify that someone's gender is female.

Ship

A term used in fan-fiction to signify which characters you ship or see as a couple in a relationship.

(Example: Captain Kirk and Spock of The Original Star Treck often used their ship to speak about their own romantic affection and loyalty to one another.)

Skoliosexual

A person attracted to non-binary, transgender and non-conforming gender identities. Or, simpler, they aren't attracted to cis-gender people.

Slur

An indistinct speech when sounds blend together.

A remark that is meant to insult, or inflict injury, by innuendo, critique or slander.

Slut

A woman who has many casual sexual partners. A derogatory term.

Social Construct

A somewhat firm idea, notion, concept or perception that is created and shared by various members of a social group who act as if their construct is something that exists even if it's not embodied in the objective reality.

Social Justice

A view that everyone in society deserves access to the same set of opportunities, rights, protections and duties.

Social Justice Warrior

It's often used in derogatory terms as in someone fighting too many battles for the sake of fighting. A person who is seen as someone easily offended and in search of a battle to engage in.

Social Role

A set of rules, behaviours, characteristics and attitudes a person holding a certain position in a certain social group must uphold to play the role given to them.

Different social groups have various levels of strictness over how these roles must be played and performed.

Each individual has many social roles for different social groups that the individual belongs to.

Sociology

A social science that studies societies, cultures, social groups, behaviours, interactions and patterns that are maintained through time preserving, or changing, the society that is consisted of them.

Spectrasexual

A person who is attracted to different labels on the spectrum of sexuality. It means they are attracted to more sexes, genders or expressions but not all of them.

Spectrum

A band of colours as seen in the rainbow.

A way to measure something that isn't set in well-defined different categories but set on a continuum without steps in slightly changing variations.

Speculation

An act of concocting a theory without any concrete proof or research.

Standard

An agreed-upon measure against which everything else like it is valued, jugged, measured.

Stealth

People who are not visibly transgender. It refers to people who, after going through the process of transition don't like to disclose their birth gender.

The controversy around the term is in its implied sense of sneakiness and dishonesty.

It's also used to refer to a gay man who "Goes under the radar". (Radar being gaydar.)

Stereotype

A fixed, generalized, oversimplified way of viewing all members of a particular group as same in some regard or manner. Thinking that all members of some group will act, behave, look, think the same way.

STD

Sexually Transmitted Diseases

Stonewall

The Stonewall Riots (uprising or rebellion) began on the 28 of June 1969 in response to a police raid at Stonewall Inn in Greenwich Village, New York.

The event is considered to be the starting point of the fight for gay liberation and LGBT+ rights.

A year after, the first gay pride march was made on the same date. Pride is celebrated in June worldwide to this day.

Straight

A person, male or female by birth who is accepting their assigned gender, attracted only to the opposite gender.

Statistics

A branch of mathematics that deals with numerical data. It's a science where people, traits, occurrences, etc., are translated into numerical values which are further studied and from which theories are drawn, proven and disproven.

Stud

A dominant lesbian. The term originated in the African-American lesbian community of the USA.

Suicide

Death caused by injuring oneself with an intention to die.

Survival Sex

A form of prostitution when people exchange sex for basic human necessities like food, shelter, a place to sleep, other basic needs, or drugs.

Systemic

Something that affects the whole rather than just parts.

Systemic Injustice

When the system as a whole is set in a way that promotes and prolongs prejudices, injustices and unfair treatment.

(Example: Laws that promote or support racism, ableism, sexism, etc.)

T

156

T4T

Trans for Trans People

A term to signify how a trans person is interested/attracted/preferring to date other trans people.

TGNC

Transgender and Gender Non-Conforming people

TERF

Trans Exclusionary Radical Feminist. Feminists that are convinced how to be a woman protected and advocated by feminism, to be included in female spaces and female discourses, one must be born and pronounced a woman at birth. It's a way to express criticism towards Trans Identities and exclude Trans Women from female spaces out of fear for the security of women feminism is trying to protect and elevate.

By extension, it furthers prejudices towards Trans Women as men in disguise preying on women.

Theory

A set of propositions, observations and conclusions that are made by thinking.

Some theories are proven by experience, experiments and observations. Other theories are suggested but still not proven. Many theories can't ever be proven.

It's a construct of the mind consistent with different ideas and interconnected events that tries to explain reality and anything in it.

Often, we act as some theory is a fact but in reality, most of the things we believe are theories and almost nothing is a fact.

They/Them

A neutral pronoun most commonly used to address Gender Non-Conforming, Agender, Non-Binary, Pangender or other gender identities, or expression.

It's to be used if a person asks you to, or you're unsure how to address them.

The argument against the usage of it is that it's not in the spirit of the language to address one person in a plural pronoun.

Third Gender

People who are defined, either by society or themselves, as neither men nor women but rather neither, both, or a combination of different characteristics.

Thon

One of the suggested neutral pronouns in the third gender that avoids mentioning or assuming someone's gender. It's meant to be used for non-binary individuals.

It's one of the first known purposefully made neutral pronouns. It's created by American composer Charles Crozat Converse in 1858.

Nominative   Thon
Accusative Thon
Pronominal Possessive   Thons
Predicative Possessive   Thon's
Reflexive   Thonself

Top

A gay man who prefers to take on a more active sexual role.

Top Surgery

A surgery of removing one's breasts, in case of a Trans Man (FTM), or surgery of making breasts, in a case of a Trans Woman (MTF).

Trancestors

Trans Elders who serve as an example to Trans People of today. The word clashes words Transgender with Ancestors to signify how Trans People who were rejected by their family have a replacement family that can guide them and provide a sense of identity.

Trans-antagonistic

A person hostile towards Trans People.

Trans Identities

People whose gender identity doesn't agree with the gender assigned at birth.

Trans Man

A man who was assigned to be a woman at birth but his inner gender identity is male.

Trans Woman

A woman who was assigned to be a man at birth but her inner gender identity is female.

Transfeminism

A branch of feminism concerned with trans issues. It states how Trans Women should be recognized for participating in issues that women face daily and that the fight to protect women and have equal rights to men includes Trans Women.

Transgender

An umbrella term that refers to any person whose inner gender identity differs from the gender assigned at birth. That includes any gender expression, the status of transition, or the lack of any kind of transition.

It encompasses different trans identities like Tran Man, Trans Woman, Non-Binary, Fluid and others.

Transition

A process of transition from the gender assigned at birth to an inner gender that that person experiences as their true gender.

The process is unique and individual for each person because each person decides for themselves how extensive their transition will be and where they feel the most comfortable on the gender spectrum. This process can last for years.

The process can include but is not limited to:

1. Social transition, where a person adjusts to social standards and rules of the gender they are transitioning to. That may include learning things society teaches people they should be/emulate/know.

2. Gender expression, where a person adjusts their appearance to the gender they are transitioning to. The goal of this stage isn't passing as the gender assigned

at birth but to express one's inner self to be reflected in the outer appearance.

3. Medical transition, this might include hormone therapy, hormone blockers, and top surgery and/or bottom surgeries.

4. Legal transition, where a persons legal ID and data is changed to be in accordance with the gender the person is transitioning into.

Transmedicalism

A belief that for someone to be a transgender that person has to experience Gender Dysphoria, and/or go through medical transition.

The belief is rooted in the need of some Trans People, who went through with medical transition and experienced years of suffering from Gender Dysphoria, to be recognized as more different than people experimenting with gender and playing on the spectrum without experiencing the suffering of being Trans.

Although it can be argued that there is a significant difference in the life experience of older generations of Trans People who suffer through adversity to get to their transition and younger people playing on the gender spectrum of identity and expression, it's argued that this belief contributes to the invalidation of Non-Binary Identities and serves as a type of Gatekeeping of the Trans Community.

Mostly, Transmedicalists belong to moderate views of asking for differentiation and recognition of their struggle.

Radical Transmedicalists can be hostile towards Non-Binary people and other, less typical, gender identities.

(Also known as a Transmed, Trumed, Trident Trans (TT), or Nunchuck Non-Binary. A pejorative label is Truscum.)

Transmisogyny

A dislike, or prejudice towards Trans Women.

Transphobia

An irrational fear, or aversion, discrimination, hostility towards Trans People.

Transsexual

A person who decided to live, and maybe, but not necessarily, undergo gender-affirming surgery, in a different gender than that assigned at birth.

The term is somewhat dubious and not liked by everyone. Use it only if asked to.

Transvestite

A term used to describe people who dress in the style of the opposite sex. Another being a crossdresser. Nowadays it's considered to be a slur or an offensive way to describe Transgender People.

Trixensexual

Attraction to women and non-binary individuals. It suggests that the person isn't attracted to masculinity without stating their own gender. (Also known as Trixenamoric.)

Trixic

A non-binary person attracted to women. They also can refer to themselves as lesbians. (Notice how in this term the gender of the person in question is in contrast to Trixensexual.)

Tucking

A process of strapping and concealing of male genitalia so they won't be seen in tight clothes while a person is displaying the feminine gender role.

Twink

A young lean gay, or a bisexual, man in his late teens or early twenties. Their appearance may include an average, or a slim, built, general attractiveness and a youthful appearance.

Two-Spirit

An Indigenous Queer Person.

U

168

Umbrella Term

A term that covers a lot more under-categories. The LGBT+ term is an umbrella term for different queer identities regardless of gender and sexuality in question. Transgender is an umbrella term for anyone who doesn't feel comfortable in their Assigned Gender, although it's under discussion how extensive that umbrella term should be.

Under the Radar

When someone isn't visibly gay.

Undetectable

A Trans Person so good at expressing the inner gender that it can't be detected just by looking at them.

Undocuqueer

A queer identity that states how the person in question is an illegal immigrant as well as queer. It adds to the layer of challenges this person faces in the world.

Uranic

A person experiencing attraction to all gender identities except those that are feminine, women or non-binary female-aligned individuals. (Notice how here the defining factor is repulsion, not attraction.)

V

172

Ve

One of the suggested neutral pronouns in the third gender that avoids mentioning or assuming someone's gender. It's meant to be used for non-binary individuals.

Nominative   Ve/Vi

Accusative Ver/Vir

Pronominal Possessive   Vis

Predicative Possessive   Vers/Virs

Reflexive   Verself/Virself

Venusic

A non-binary identifying person attracted exclusively to women, women-aligned persons and Lunarians. (Notice how this term states the gender in question and their exclusive sexual orientation, unlike the term Trixic that doesn't state exclusivity.)

Verse

A gay man who's ready to switch roles in sexual intercourse.

Voguing

A highly stylized form of dance that expressed queerness created by black and Latino LGBTQ communities. The name was inspired by the magazine Vogue.

176

Woman

A gender category that is defined through rules and expression of femininity. It usually entails traits like gentleness, kindness, beauty, sadness, long hair, painted nails, skirts, dresses, jewellery, high heels and other signifiers of outer expressing. Within biology, it's signified with the ability to birth children, breastfeed and menstruate. Having a vagina and breasts is also one of the tell signs of a female. Still, even if you spot all mentioned above, caution is advised. In this day and age, you never can tell for sure.

(Side note: I'm well aware that this definition alone can be rage-inducing but in the lack of other signifiers it's hard to determine a woman without resorting to biology, or emotions. At least, I didn't succumb in listing things a woman can or can not do.)

(Side-side note: This description is based on the current Western expression of the female gender role. We should be aware that in other parts of the globe women don't wear jewellery and their clothes are defined differently, and high heels were a fashion for men when they were invented.)

WLW

Women Loving Women

An acronym to signify a preference women have in their sexual attraction not revealing the other parts of one's identity.

WSW

Women who have Sex with Women

A medical term that doesn't refer to sexual orientation, or identity, but focuses on sexual intercourses a woman could have.

X-Chromosome

A chromosome most humans have. If it's paired with a Y-chromosome it defines male sex characteristics to emerge in humans. If it's paired with another X-chromosome it defines female characteristics to emerge.

Xe

One of the suggested neutral pronouns in the third gender, which avoids mentioning or assuming someone's gender. It's meant to be used for non-binary individuals.

Nominative	Xe
Accusative	Xem
Pronominal Possessive	Xyr
Predicative Possessive	Xyrs
Reflexive	Xemself

Xena the Warrior Princess

The character in a titular show.

Xenogender

An umbrella term for non-binary gender identities that don't use the usual terminology that language provides us with for describing gender.

A series of non-binary gender identities that don't relate to binary social gender at all. People who fall under this umbrella can relate and identify with any object, concept or idea.

Xenophobia

An irrational, or exaggerated fear, hostility or aversion towards foreigners, strangers or foreign and strange things.

184

Y-Chromosome

A chromosome in humans that determines male sex. It's usually paired with an X-chromosome but it has variants where multiple Y-chromosome's appear.

Z

188

Ze

One of the suggested neutral pronouns in the third gender, which avoids mentioning or assuming someone's gender. It's meant to be used for non-binary individuals.

Nominative   Ze
Accusative Zir
Pronominal Possessive   Zir
Predicative Possessive   Zirs
Reflexive   Zirself

Speculation

Aka, things we think may be the truth but are not proven by facts. The process of guessing the true nature of the universe.

192

Tools:

Aka, things we use to operate on other things, to fix, dismantle or create them.

194

Words and How We Use Them

If you scrolled through this dictionary, you might have noticed that there are words in the dictionary that seem out of place, that don't belong in the dictionary of Queer Culture.

To understand what is being said you must understand the words used. I didn't want to presume people coming in to read a light read of Queer Culture know, or know for sure, what the meaning is of the more complex words I'm using to express a thought.

More than that, I wanted to be understood how I use those words in this context.

Putting aside the knowledge of the words we do, or do not, possess, Queer Culture exists in the context of the culture that surrounds us. We're not divided and separated from the world in a small box of completely different labels and content.

Words such as emotions, experience and behaviour apply to us as much as to people who don't fit in any of the many boxes we made for ourselves to jump between. (To make ourselves less crowded and to diminish the sense of a restriction one box may have.)

The context of words the wider social constructs are using is also applicable to us. We still have other social roles and aren't limited to our Queer Identity.

Still, it's fun to have one when you're the one who gets to write the label on the lid, isn't it?

Occam's Razor and When to Use it

A rule in philosophy credited to William Ockham. It states that there should be no unnecessary multiplying of the idea when seeking truth.

"It is futile to do with more what can be done with fewer," was what Ockham actually said.

The rule was over-simplified with time, as things usually are, reducing his complex thought to a formula that the simpler, more elegant solution, is closer to the truth.

The truth of biology, and sociology, is that it's more common to add up complexity over time than to retract it. We still wear our appendixes around even if we might die from them at any moment and they serve no apparent purpose in our bodies.

"It is futile to do with more what can be done with fewer," states a really important condition.

"When it can be done with fewer."

In cases that it can't be done with fewer, it should be done with as many ingredients as it has to be.

Many people resist the multitude of queer labels labelling them unnecessary and excessive. Still, for those using those labels, they stoped being restrictive stereotypes but instead become almost therapeutic tools that explain our state of being to ourselves as much as to those who seek counsel with us wanting to connect to us as rational human beings able to express ourselves.

The multitude of labels exists since there's no coherent group of queer people gathering on the same place at the same time. The same thing we may notice in the general society. Many of labels are used to describe different types of women, mothers, men, fathers, children, employees and all sorts of different social roles.

There shouldn't be any shame to exchange and own some labels of our own even if the broader social construct is sometimes mocking us as snowflakes for it.

Still, Occam's Razor is a useful tool to consider.

When in need, consider which of your many labels is suitable to simply explain yourself in a necessary manner revealing only things you're ready to expose in a certain social situation.

The larger Queer Passport that helps you decide and navigate the complicated life that is queer experience hold dear as a tool of mental health and your secret magical name that defines you in terms you're comfortable with.

Luhman's theory of simplification

Now, there is a need for me to read Luhman again. You must understand that I'm old and I got my degree in Sociology over a decade ago so my interpretation may differ. That's why, don't accredit Luhman any mistakes or poor interpretation but to my flawed memory (and the fact that I studied in a different language than English).

Here, again, we face simplicity.

It's a theory that people when face the growing complexity of social constructs resort to simplification.

It's a simple idea of simplification.

Human's minds are lazy, we are hard to remember all the fact about something so we remember only a few redacted ideas that represent the grand complex idea.

It means that the broader society will inevitable restrict queer experience to this stereotype or another. They won't have the patience to keep the whole complexity of variations in their mind. It's not important enough to occupy their mental space reserved for grocery lists and timetables of the school schedule.

Don't judge them too severely, or yourself if you're the one of the majority reading this book about a minority language (in that case I applaud your effort to fight off conformism), we are all like that. You probably won't remember the whole assembly of a football team, or if you would, you won't know something else that is crucial to other people.

In our daily lives, we all have different priorities and different ideas are valuable enough to us to memorise them in their totality. I, for example, don't expect of me to know all these terms by heart after I exit this book. I don't even remember the names of all of the characters I spent years building. The mind must be cleared to perform and contain the new project that is ahead.

Still, even if it's a stereotype and it's simplified, we can strive to make our stereotypes better, to press in using shame, compassion, understanding and other methods to assert our presence and show our colours.

When the dust settles, if we win our spot under the protection of the law, it won't matter what some individuals think of you if you know you're protected before the law as much as they are.

That doesn't have to be much, law is a flawed machine created and governed by people, but it's the same thing the next person has. It's the thing we can achieve.

For the things we can't achieve, there's some tomorrow and some new kids we'll watch with awe and horror as they think of something we would never approve of. Then, when we find ourselves accused of being old, rigid, and, god-forbid, conservative, we'll have a fun experience of making the whole journey of life.

Queer Curves and Meaning of Life

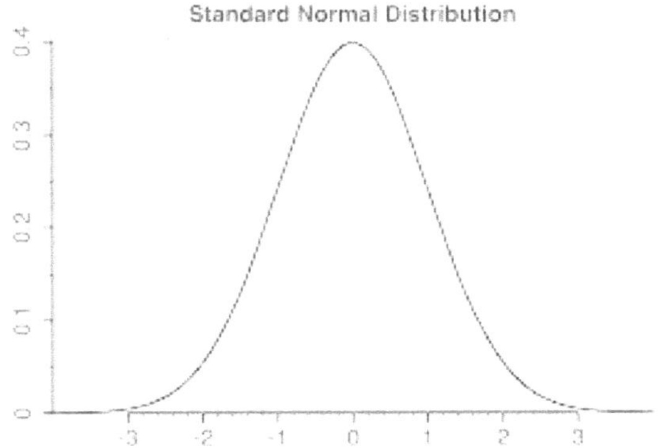

This is the Gauss Curve or the normal distribution. Its shape should be the way any random statistical data will gather. That is the theory, the way random numbers operate.

If you take a group of people, ask them questions most of the answers will lay somewhere in the middle and the least of them will end up on the edge of the spectrum. That's why minorities are minorities. They have extreme views that don't conform to the worldview of the majority.

So, the working theory, the one we would have to prove through data if we're researchers, would be that on the spectrum of two opposing binary characteristics most of the people will end up at the middle of the spectrum and the further we go from the centre the lesser our group of people will be.

Queer Culture loves to use the word spectrum but it's sometimes difficult to establish what are the opposing points of the spectrum and how the dots in between are set.

It's very different, the data you expect to get if you propose different opposing points spectrum is consisted off.

I'll give you a preposterous example.

Let's say that the spectrum of sexuality is set of two points, the point of asexuality on one side and sexuality on the other, just by setting those two opposing points we would make an assumption that in any random group of people the majority of subjects would fall somewhere in the middle having characteristics of fluid sexuality where they are sometimes experiencing spikes of asexuality and sometimes spikes of sexuality.

By doing so, we made an assumption that the majority of humans aren't completely sexual, that they don't experience sexual attraction regularly but rather occasionally.

By our own labels, that would put more people on the Asexual Spectrum than one would expect.

I'll give you another example, maybe an easier one.

If we make a spectrum consisting of two opposing points where one is homosexuality, attraction to the same sex, and the other one is heterosexuality, attraction to the opposite sex. It's quite easy to see that if we set our values that way our middle would be bisexuality, attraction towards the opposite and the same sex. That would mean the majority of people are bisexual, minorities would be straights and gays, people attracted only to one gender.

You might notice that our expected results would greatly vary on our offered working theory we would have to prove or disprove through research and gathering statistical data.

Of course, in our society it's just assumed that the middle of the bell consists of straight people but if that is so, what would be the extreme points of that bell? On one side monosexual people, on other multisexual people, but that wouldn't work since heterosexual people are by definition monosexual people. When opposing points would be monosexual-multisexual we would again end up with a bisexual middle.

What else could it be?

I guess I'm biased because I already believe the majority is bisexual but dislikes to talk or think about it. My bias prevents me from seeing probably obvious options where heterosexuality would be the logical middle.

Moving on.

With gender, there is a similar problem. How to get a spectrum where being cisgendered would be an expected mathematical middle?

If we put opposing points to be persons without gender against people with too many genders, Agender-Multigender, what would be the middle? Maybe there it would be the cisgender middle, but it would be more likely just binary gender in the middle whatever that one gender you're experiencing may be, including Trans Women and Trans Men who are quite sure their gender is a singular one. There in the middle, there wouldn't be any discrimination in numbers distinguishing who is trans and who is not, the only question would be doing you feel you have gender and how many genders you experience.

Another proposed spectrum of gender might be entertaining the thought that gender is indeed binary and that we have only two options of gender. Then we would end up with opposing points being Female and the opposing one Male. Then the middle would be people who can't decide what gender they are. We would end up with the proposition that the majority of people are in fact non-binary. That they don't feel their gender so strongly to identify just with one side of the spectrum. That the majority of people have traits of both genders.

In that case, Trans People who are sure they belong to the opposite side would be as rare as people who strongly connect to their assigned gender. The majority would look at them confused why they consider gender so real when it's hard to distinguish which characteristics are manly and which womanly.

You can see by the proposed options that possible outcomes might vary on the questions we are asking but that's the power and the limitation of science.

Science studies work that way. There are proposed working theories asking questions that are set-up by those theories. They are proven and disproven by research data. Still, we must consider that in return questions often shape the answers. The way questions are put is likely to influence the answer the subject will give.

If we never ask different questions, we can't ever get different answers.

If the choice is always the same, the answer is always the same and more often than not, the answer is the one that is expected of us rather than that we thought through and gained knowledge of it through questioning, experience and observation.

Especially since human life isn't conducted like a science experiment. People are living their lives by pre-set rules they followed because they were taught so.

Maybe the biggest difference between the Queer Culture as a minority and the surrounding majority cultures is that the Queer Culture is an experiment. It's a way of life that is led through questioning, experimenting, thinking and constantly creating new theories of gender, identity and sexuality to try out.

That way the Queer Culture is constantly changing challenging the surrounding society to adapt, to fight and to change to something new, something a bit different.

As in any fight between David and the Goliath, the slight rock can get you a win but never expect that the win will grant you everything you're bargaining for.

In an experiment, many takes fail, theories get abandoned, or disproved. No matter the obstacles, to gain deeper knowledge and understand human nature better we must persist.

Because that is the conclusion of this small Queer ABC. The Queer Culture is the philosophical exploration of human nature, an experiment on people, conducted by people for their own gain of freedom and sense of fulfilment.

Closeted Fiction:

Aka, fiction that uses queerness without exposing it to the general public. In short, it exposes general audiences to queerness without ever admitting to it.

Sherlock Holmes and John Watson, or They Were Roommates

We don't have to be all serious down here. After all, we're queer, which means skewed, and gay, which means happy.

It doesn't have to all be gloom and doom even if we're fighting in trenches demanding some rights that should already be ours.

There are fun things like a life we have inside of fiction and examining some old familiar faces to see that they too have secret Queer Passports others refuse to see.

Examination of fiction isn't reserved only to those who are attracted to their characters but can also serve for us to see ourselves reflected in some archetypical heroes. It's a way for our sub-consciousness to see how we can make choices that are heroic and not villainous. An indirect way to fight that pesky internalized self-phobia that makes us act against our best interest.

One of those characters is the legendary Sherlock Holmes. The one everyone has heard of. Even when he was created, in the prude Victorian era, his housing arrangement rose eyebrows making its readers at the time question his sexuality.

It was unbecoming for mature men to be unmarried and live together. Stories of Sherlock Holmes were the first ones to receive attention in a form of fan-fiction.

Even the first fan petition to revive the series was held for two years because of the death of beloved Sherlock. His author, Arthur Conan Doyle, hated his character enough to give him an unfair death just to be able to stop writing him.

Still, after two years of persistent letters that didn't stop coming in, he succumbed and revived the character without any explanation to show off his grumpiness about it.

So, Sherlock Holmes and John Watson were roommates and even in the age where it shouldn't be even mentioned it rose suspicions about their sexuality.

'They were roommates,' is a somewhat mocking phrase that shows various historians refusing to see the queer context even when it's blatantly written out in form of passionate and erotic letters.

I came across an article that established how Leonardo Da Vinci was proven to be ambidextrous, left-handed and gay. I never heard anyone speaking about that in the general public, but then again, maybe I just live in an outback of the world. I know I do, it's deliberate that this is a place such things are never talked about.

Still, Sherlock Holmes and his roommate John Watson shared a life of adventure and adrenaline all the while living in the same house, maybe even the same room as a random sentence might suggest in the original text but those are just speculations. Those are fictional characters and we can't tell what happened in the unwritten pages or didn't happen.

Yet, there's no shame in taking those characters to our lines to make a mosaic of values we, as queer people, can follow while creating our own patterns in the universe.

Hija de la fortuna, Travelling the world Crossdressed

Daughter of Fortune by a wonderful writer with impeccable style Isabela Allende was such a pleasant surprise when I found it.

At the time, I wasn't actively thinking of my gender or was aware of the complexities behind my gender expression. Yet, even unaware, I was in awe before our heroine who walked the world cross-dressed as a man shaping her own destiny rather than submitting to the one that was unacceptable to her.

Watching the world over her shoulder, her not challenging gender but still, challenging gender expression, the world changed before her allowing her to travel on her own in the time when that was too dangerous for a woman to do.

Yet, her companion of Asian disposition revealed to me my unconscious prejudice towards a romantic hero. Just for the fact that he was Asian at that time and place, I didn't consider him, or the things he does as romantic at all.

You must excuse me and my limited upbringing. But that made me think some more about the infamous white straight male hero who has to be the centre of any adventure for it to be valued as important.

To cure my lack of exposure to Asian people, to the culture I was exposed through the books I loved to read, I went and submerged myself in the Korean world of series. It was wonderful. I recommend it as love therapy any day.

A Korean sense of romance is somewhat pure and their shows really prude but I come from a similar country and I appreciate the safety of their stories.

Still, it was a surprise to discover just how many stories about queer gender, crossdressing and even fluidity I managed to find. Of course, like in Croatia, they tend to pretend that there is nothing queer about those stories. That those are just people who happen to fall into the situation where they just have to cross-dress.

I accept even that in the lack of better representation. I maybe even prefer it over a direct way queerness is portrayed in Western Media where it seems that to be queer is to suffer, be generally miserable or die, mostly to die.

Tajna krvavog mosta, Croatian Trans Narative

Croatian novel about a crossdresser is written by the Croatian most famous author Marija Jurić Zagorka. She was a notorious feminist, the first female political journalist in Eastern Europe. All and all a fierce woman who shaped her own destiny gaining fame and fortune in the day and age where most women were bound to their home.

The novel, The Secret of The Bridge of Blood, maybe the most famous Croatian novel to date, followed a young woman forced by an older woman to dress up as a man, live as a man, go around in the company of men to spy on a man for her.

Nobody ever talks about the fact that the said man when he fell in love, fell in love with a young man and was quite distraught about it. On top of that, he was quite clearly codded as a gay man from the start with the constant overstating of how he resists the charms of women and prefers to spend his days drinking with his buddies.

Even the relief he experiences when he finds out how the target of his affection isn't a young man but a woman is short-lived to be replaced with disgruntled dissatisfaction because he misses his friend.

That trouble resolves itself only when his now-wife agrees to dress up as a man from time to time to spice up their life.

It sounds all really straightforward, doesn't it? It's queer as it can get. It's not even secluded, nor did he fall in love after he finds out her true gender as it happens in similar stories like it.

Still, nobody ever acknowledges there's anything slightly queer about that story that includes practices as binding breasts, making an effort to pass as a man, questioning one's sexuality and using cross-dressing to improve one's marriage.

The queerness of it is invisible to the general audience that unapologetically adores this classic of Croatian fiction.

Queer erasure is strong in us.

Even I, when I read it for the first time as a young teen, didn't think of it as queer. Only when I revisited it as an adult did I pause and wonder.

I guess, nothing short of showing off genitalia will classify as queer beyond the shred of doubt. No wonder so many shows about queer people are so sexualized. To make the viewer believe the characters on screen sharing kisses and holding hands are more than just good friends or roommates.

Jeeves and Wooster in a Closet

Speaking of the closet, Jeeves and Wooster literally end up hiding in the closet before the relentless pursuit of women Wooster has no desire to marry for no apparent reason but that he doesn't want to marry.

A British show, if you haven't heard of it, Jeeves and Wooster is an absolute gem you must experience. It's a must on a queer to-watch list.

Played by the irreplaceable Steven Fry, an openly gay man, and hilarious Hugh Laurie younger generations might identify as serious Doctor House but we older people know him as a goofy and ridiculously funny comedic actor that ruled British comedy once upon a time.

The story begins when a notorious bachelor Wooster who spends his days drinking with his buddies and not thinking of marriage (sounds familiar?) gets a new valet Jeeves who practically imposes himself as his servant moving in and taking over Wooster's daily life without a pause making him completely dependent upon his services.

The story progresses in the same manner. Wooster gets into this trouble or that one and Jeeves finds a clever way to escape it. The trouble most commonly being some stranded woman wanting to marry unsuspecting Wooster who fears marriage like nothing else.

For many, they are probably just the best of chums even if they, Hugh and Steven, played on and with gayness in their sketches very directly and not subtly at all. For me, the best feel-good gay romance you can come across that solely focuses on the relationship and feelings of its main protagonists.

Exploration Fiction:

Aka, fiction that explores queer topics through general models, archetypical journeys, openly queer characters and settings. It suggests queerness to the general audience directly as a valid alternative option of living.

Virginia Wolf, Orlando and Gender Fluidity

Orlando is wonderful.

No, not Orlando Bloom, although he too is arguably wonderful, Orlando from the infamous and brilliant author Virginia Wolf.

Virginia Wolf is one of those wonderful authors who left enough of written evidence behind that even most stubborn supporters of 'they were roommates' consider her as a queer, probably lesbian, or maybe bisexual, woman.

Judging by Orlando, maybe her gender was queer too but that can't be but speculation.

I read Orlando fairly young and was really happy when I found it. To see the movie where Tilda Swinton interprets Orlando was a neat reminder of the wonder that is that book.

Orlando is so unapologetically fluid in their gender.

Since it's a piece of fiction, when they transition to a woman, she can receive a magical full transition that even allows her the full scope of female experience through a pregnancy.

Just to witness Orlando's changing sex without engaging in any form of justification of that act was refreshing, freeing and made me laugh.

Try it, maybe it makes you laugh, but I don't remember it so clearly. All I remember is Tilda putting the layered manuscript on the table.

Memories are like that, they diminish and simplify the layered experience to a few lines or an image.

I don't mind that process. When I was young I had perfect memory but you can't create anything from clear recollection, you can just reproduce. That's why I diminished my focus on recollecting and let my memories get pressed until only the fresh, strong and clear memories remain.

I discovered that I had the right kind of theory.

From the pressed in dry leaves, new patterns could be drawn quite nicely.

Kafka and the Sense of Otherness

Do you remember reading Kafka? Or rather yet, do you have to read Kafka as your high-school read?

We did. It's something I would never read on my own, as many mandatory reads are. Still, I'm glad I have those stories pressed in the herbarium of my memory. It's an interesting one.

The Kafkaesque feeling of those stories is easily recognizable in any context. Just recently I bought a small game for my son. He refused to play it because it was drawn like a nightmare and I suddenly recognized the Kafkaesque quality of the drawing.

The sense of otherness Kafka gave to the world is quite a unique one. The metamorphosis into a cockroach out of all things. (I know, research told me it's a huge insect, it's not specified as a cockroach but yet my mind envisions it like that just like many adaptations chose that form too as probably the most disturbing out of choices of insects.)

But the sense of otherness Kafka gave to the world can relate to the queer experience of being a stranger to one's own body, to be hated and distrusted by your surroundings. To a general feeling of alienation.

I have no idea where to go with this. Probably because I never fell in love with Kafka but it's nice to have something like that out there that causes discomfort and makes people question, re-examine and doubt their sense of identity even if it is just for a few pages.

For an end note: Try not to fall into the abyss of otherness where it starts to seem everyone is strange and that the world is a dark place set up against us. It's hard to climb out of that abyss. Watch trees from time to time to see beauty is still there no matter how the sense of otherness and alienation can creep into our daily routines.

Bujold and a Hermaphrodite

Now, let's be clear, I simply adore Bujold. Lois McMaster Bujold is everything. She gave me a life where everything else seemed dull and unexciting.

Miles Vorkosigan is the best hero I can think of.

His saga is the thing to enjoy.

Still, after this intro, you just know there is a problem. A small problem in a form of a hermaphrodite and no, it's not for the usage of the word that is now considered offensive. It wasn't considered offensive once upon a time and I don't have a contextual experience that would make that word negatively charged for me personally.

I didn't even notice that problem when I first read the saga as it went out freshly pressed from the printing press in Croatian translation. I just read on confident that even if I dislike some aspects of it, the author will fix it eventually.

I remember exiting the saga somewhat disappointed but at the time it was just a sense, meh, straight romances. He could have done better.

It was when I read it again recently in a worn-out English edition. More precisely, I re-read the stories that contained my one and only favourite Bel Thorne the hermaphrodite. I adored that character through and through.

It was painful to read it in the English version because all the scenes between them, Miles and Bel, were more charged, there was more subtext, it was romantic and there was tension. Of course, Croatian translation failed to convey the nuance, probably not due to the translator but the strict nature of Croatian language that isn't the most romantic language you'll find.

But worse than that, I came to the end of Bel's story and discovered that it wasn't fixed, that Bel was left like that, broken, injured and defeated in the middle of the saga never to be seen again.

That made me so angry that I could scream. Instead of screaming, I went to write and that anger you have to thank or resent, the mere existence of saga Onlookers and its unapologetic explicit queerness. I don't want to hear about any confusion or accusations that they were just very good friends.

Torchwood and Raging Omnisexuality

Yes, I'm well aware that Captain Jack Harkness comes into life through Doctor Who but in Doctor Who he's always sugar-coated and his sexuality is diminished to introduction phrase that goes nowhere.

More importantly, I watched Torchwood first and only through it got addicted to Doctor Who so for me Torchwood always comes as a primary fiction, the source code.

Don't get angry with me, it's just like when people walk into Middle Earth through Lord of the Rings and think of Hobbit as a prequel. I don't go around getting angry about that.

For you who didn't watch either, it's not everyone's cup of tea but Torchwood is the epitome of unbound sexual orientation that isn't limited or governed by labels of any kind.

Main characters, not just Jack, get into steamy situations with different genders and alien species without anyone making any kind of a deal out of it.

Lead by Captain Jack Harkness, whose "real name" we never get to know. Nor his original gender since he mentions casually he was pregnant at least once in his long life.

This show is a true gem to me since it displays queerness for all to see without discussing, labelling or being burdened by it.

Maybe because it is sci-fi that is still set in our day and age makes it even better. It serves as a small pocket of wickedness and questions morality with hard hitting dilemmas that aren't so easily answered.

It exposes the monstrosity inside of ordinary people and humanity hidden in monsters.

It questions the world.

Maybe that's what I like the most about it. It questions not offering easy answers.

You can accuse this show for drawing me in to try in for a size a new language and a different culture. That's the value of fiction. You can never know what the outreach of it will be and how it will impact the world in which it lands.

The impact some art will have is unpredictable. Like many authors who authored unconsciously queer narratives that fight any form of xenophobia experienced themselves. Those authors often try to fight against the unintended message behind their creation but creations are like that, uncontrollable and as soon as you make them, as soon as you put them out in the world they gain a life of their own independent on their creator.

Just like us, independent upon our creator trying out different sizes to see how far our free will stretches before the heaven smites us in smithereens.

Isn't it thrilling?

I can understand with ease how fearful that makes law-abiding citizens who believe in the world end. But since we lived in caves our society progressed by sending out small group of people out in the danger to see is there anything edible out there.

It's the way the society grows. A small group of people risks with something new. If they survive, the rest of the group adapts some of new behaviours. If they die, the substance is proclaimed deadly.

In queer context, Queer Culture is the set of small groups trying out behaviours that are considered deadly, poisonous and rage inducing to see is there a way to implement those behaviours and in what way.

In the case of fiction, Torchwood was probably that small group where they freely tried out exposing sexuality to the viewer to see what will happen.

Maybe the moderate success of it produced some small queer stories all around British television-verse like Gentleman Jack and such. But British television-verse was always more inclusive and less skittish before queerness than other television-verses I noticed.

When Torchwood attempted its transplantation to USA television-verse it failed spectacularly. The gritty sexuality was gone to be replaced by world level of sacrificial pain.

I guess that USA television-verse still accepts any kind of queerness only if their queers suffer a great deal. That, I find quite unacceptable.

From their television-verse, Xena: Warrior Princess remained as a grand example of visible queerness although, by the general audience, it would probably belong to the closeted section more likely. Even if I don't see how since there was even an on-screen kiss shown between two female leads.

Still, even this show can be categorised in the plain of sacrificial efforts to redeem oneself.

A message that suffering is needed to justify your queerness really got tired and old by now.

Questioning Gender:

Aka, thinking of all things gender related. Yes, even those wretched things we dislike to think about.

The Wasteland of Gender

I was a presumptuous conceded child.

Aware of my superior smarts, assured by the mirror that my aesthetic is symmetric enough to be considered pretty and that there was nothing about my body that would stand out in a way to make me unappealing.

There was no reason for me to feel anything but good about myself.

And I did feel good about myself satisfied with my scores and my friends.

Still, I did observe that my appearance, attitude, speech, something was making people squirm from discomfort when faced with me. I noticed that there isn't a lot of approval around me, except for the recognition of my smarts so I took it that people are maybe intimidated by my smarts.

And maybe they were, who knows what's in other people's heads.

I also observed that my looks were never considered as something to compliment or notice. That I was treated like I wasn't pretty at all.

That baffled me.

The mirror showed the aesthetics of my face but it wasn't received as such by my surroundings. No one thought of me as endearing, or cute.

Intimidating was the most common signifier, even if it wasn't said, it was rarely said, but it could be seen in the posture and tone of the voice of people speaking to me.

I got used from an early age to be treated like that, like someone you should be careful with. Someone you avoid or refrain from revealing too much of yourself.

I had enough friends who didn't mind me to be bothered by that reaction. I didn't think of it almost at all. Most of the time I thought that was the normal way to be treated. Only when some of my friends would get upset with someone I would notice that there was something strange in the way people treated me, or, more commonly, constantly stared at me.

I thought it was normal for everyone to stare at you.

I thought it was because I'm loud. Or because I dress up flashy and noticeable.

I didn't care either way.

The first time I encountered the thought that I could be a man was at the end of grade school. We learned about gender and gender differences.

There were categories of characteristics and behaviours and in the set-up, I was presented with, I was predominately put in the male category. I didn't think of it much but as I was taught more about gender roles the more I noticed how most of my traits end up on the male side of the aisle.

I explained that to myself by statistics. "In statistics, the difference within a gender is greater than those between them," what the go-to phrase I used to explain the discrepancy later on in high school.

But there and then on the hallways of my grade school, I thought of the possibility that I was a man and the world where everyone like me would be considered to be men.

I disliked the idea dearly.

The idea enraged me.

It was like cheating.

I said to my friend there and then that it was unfair. It's not ok for men to take all the qualities they deem as more valuable and claim them for themselves. It's the shortest and best way to gain an advantage and claim supremacy over women. If every and any woman with my disposition would declare to be a man, then women would be left only with individuals with demure and soft features, they would be truly unprotected and left at the mercy of men without any anger, or aggression within themselves to fight off men and assert their rights.

It wasn't said in exactly such a manner, it was said in Croatian, but the gist of it is about the same. Even then I spoke like that like I'm giving out speeches at conferences to concerned crowds about important issues. I was preoccupied with issues of the world, ecology, justice, right and all such notions.

After a lifetime of experience, I still didn't leave that initial stance. I won't change my sex to appease the world and fit neatly into the right category and stopped being stared at.

I'm spiteful like that.

I did try out presenting myself as a man when I finally came around to entertain the idea of the life lived as a man. When I present myself as a man, no one stares at me. No one notices anything strange about me. Men nod when they pass me by, they ask me to carry stuff with them. Although some did yell fagot after me, most of the people were quite indifferent towards my outer appearance.

My life experience taught me that there is some basis for the distribution of male and female characteristics in categories. Most people I met felt quite satisfied and content inside of the protection of their gender which I considered as a constraint.

My stance shifted a bit towards the belief that it's not about the distribution of traits but the way society views those traits. These days I think we should reprogram ourselves to see traditionally female characteristics to hold as much value as male ones.

That stance made me less presumptuous and proud of my male characteristics. It made me see my shortcomings as a man. To see where I'm stupid because I'm a man. Where I lack perspective and nuance, where my approach is too aggressive and why I struggle so much with being a mother.

It gave me a dose of humility I always wanted to possess.

Don't get me wrong, that doesn't make me humble. I'm still as vain and proud as I can be. I have to be. It's a protective shell of sorts where I give myself validation I didn't receive from the world.

I think that is the point of Queer Pride. Pride is considered to be a sin in the major population but we have to have pride in ourselves when most often others don't have pride in us and who we are.

That's why I do understand TERF's and where they are coming from. I too see the wasteland female gender can face if we remove all rebellious, harsh, unforgiving, relentless, aggressive, unkind, firm, sturdy and strong elements from it and give in return soft, emotional, gentle, sweet, refined, elegant segments in return.

It's a sure way to assert dominance to occupy only one side.

More so, I think that they are women like me who suffered through the process of adapting to circumstances they don't like and emerged liking the process of adjusting, liking the place they ended up in, liking the person they have become.

Maybe they are afraid others won't get the same opportunity to suffer through and find rewards like children and grandchildren on the other end.

My personal belief is that most of them are just selfish women fearing they won't get to be grandmothers for this new wave that's pushing their daughters to flee to the male gender they too wished to flee to and get an easier life of privilege.

Still, I don' fear that.

I think that the process of transition is hard, it takes courage, it brings pain and requires sacrifices. I don't believe many have the endurance to go through with it.

I think that the appeal of the opposite sex will diminish by the accessibility of the same and only the most persistent ones in grave need will go through the gate of transition.

That is my belief of what will happen but my predictions are more often wrong than not.

I don't fear people transitioning or the possibility of transitioning existing easily accessible to all. Maybe because I'm a spiteful person and I know first-hand what spite can make you do just to prove a point.

Some of us are like that, we like challenges and dislike being told what to do, what to wear, how to act and how to be. For us, it's always better to have an option, to be allowed to choose differently than not to. Then it's easier to bear the choice we already made.

I guess I am selfish in the end. Sometimes to find where you're selfish you have to be honest with yourself. Then it's easier to manage your own prejudice, spite and resentment. Things we do have in great supply even if we were targets of it. Maybe, even more, when we were targets of it, those are sentiments we can easily understand and give them back to the world to see their own mirror image.

Queerness and Fertility

We had fun with graphs, didn't we?

Fun that might upset some but that's research for you. To gain truth you sometimes must propose theories you think are false to prove them wrong. Without proving some theory wrong all you have presumptions. By definition, living a life based in presumptions leads to a life of prejudice.

Of course, since our minds are prone to simplification, we will inevitably always lead a life of prejudice. It's our way of coping with the growing complexity of the world before us.

Still, we can be careful and not let our prejudice be harmful, hateful or damaging to the world around us, to people around us.

One of those prejudices is that the majority of the population is consisted of straight cisgendered people.

That is probably the most likely theory since sexuality and fertility aren't categories created by society. Unlike gender, which is a socially defined category, it's not a mathematical model that has to obey the normal distribution but a biological one.

Biological models aren't measured by statistical mathematical models. At least not with curves and spectrums. Biological models are highly discriminatory and primarily focused on the prolongation of the species, raising young and life persisting in general.

It will favour one characteristic over others if it benefits survival to the point where that characteristic becomes a danger for survival. Like horns on some antelopes growing into their skulls because females prefer long horns so much.

In the biological model, there's no diversity and fairness. You can lose your spot in the line-up of survival because your feathers aren't blue enough, let alone other characteristics.

For nature, sexuality is highly discriminatory.

It's governed by one goal only and that is procreation.

To gain sex from the opposite sex you have to fit the bill, be what the hormones and genes in us want to send out into the future.

In contrast, for nature, fertility is non-discriminatory. If you have it, nature will make you go through the labour, pains, grievances of your cubs, you'll sacrifice your safety for your chicks to grow up. You'll go hungry, you'll fight off men, and your sole goal will be to care for your young.

The hormones make sure you're madly in love with your offspring.

That is for species like us whose younglings are defenceless beings that would die on their own.

For species that has resilient new-borns that can manage on their own, attachment for your young isn't as important. What's more important is that the female gets away and gets ready to bear a new batch of creatures as soon as possible.

How does this connect to queerness?

It connects because queerness disconnects sexuality from fertility. Some see that as proof of unnatural nature (the pun) of queerness but I would argue that it probably has something to do with numbers.

We, as species, grew in numbers enough for our survival not to be in question, more so, for the survival of other life to be in question because of our numbers. Queerness is probably a safety mechanism against overpopulation. When numbers get large, statistically, queerness is bound to appear.

In large families with many children, it's just mathematically more probable that some of those children will be queer.

Of course, we as smart beings refusing to be parented and limited by pesky nature we got to ideas which grant queer people fertility.

Lesbians are in the best position here. They just need to supply themselves with an easy sample produced in large quantities by many and they are good to go. To be mothers.

Gays are at a disadvantage. They need a willing donor who is conscious (hopefully, this is the terrible world we live in) of their donation, the assistance of doctors and a painful amount of papyrology.

That is in countries you can gain access to those things. Some of us aren't so lucky. Those possibilities are somewhere accessible only to straight couples who can't bear children for this reason or another.

In a place like this one, if you are a gay man, you can't even hope to adopt a child let alone anything else.

With these two examples (in places that allow it) we have clear cut situations where participants control their destiny as parents and can get means to obtain the biological imperative to prolong the species.

With Trans People, things get trickier.

For a Trans Person to gain a child, they would have to suffer through puberty and then some more to preserve their fertile cells, go through the labouring task of creating children and only after that consider the transition.

If they go through with the transition at an early age, the option of having offspring that is biologically theirs is most likely completely lost because infertility is often a side-effect of transition.

That's where the grievance about early transition hits the fan.

Are children really capable of understanding the price of not having children who are biologically yours?

Is that a price they are able to understand?

Society says yes somewhere, and strong no elsewhere. It depends on which side of the globe you're standing on.

For now, this is the social experiment western countries are currently doing.

We'll see the outcome in the future. Will everyone follow their suit or will they be flooded by lawsuits of grownups who think their human rights were violated.

Here the question' is gender divided from sex' gets heated. Is gender identity free of the question of fertility? Is gender identity unconnected to sexuality?

Fertility is always a question of sexuality. That is until our science finds a way to divorce the two but for now they are in an explosive marriage.

To decide one's gender is to decide one's future sexuality, fertility and identity.

The argument that we need to protect children from hardship and grievance of facing adversity their challenged gender will pose for them as they grow up (they because I'm not a child anymore) sounds plausible until you think about it some more and understand that adversity and challenges are what growing up and maturing is all about.

To grant early transition to a whole generation of young Trans People might not sound bad to some who understand that is a whole generation of Trans People without children of their own.

It's a hard pill to swallow. But when you establish the right for the early transition to prevent psychological problems, then you establish that parents who oppose the transition of their children are in fact abusing said children. That grants someone with the right to remove their authority over their children.

Who then gets the authority? A child that barely understands the world and the consequences of their choices? Or the state that is just a machine made by men, or medical experts?

It's a thin thread to follow.

There should be an option of an early transition, or at least I think it should, but I would much rather avoid the scenario where the state is the one in control of determination whose gender is so challenged to be changed.

More so, just the mere required measure for your gender to be changed is to be distressed about it to the point of suicide. Isn't that a way to send young stubborn spiteful people filled with hormones afraid of the world a message that they need to be greatly distressed to get what they want?

You can sense here that I too am a concerned mother. We, mothers, are a notorious bunch who think having children is a biological imperative everyone will desire at some point in their lives.

Our perspective might be challenging but it's not invalid. To raise a child means to understand that adversity, challenges and hardships are necessary for your child to grow, mature and learn what it is for them to be adult humans.

Not that we should give them adversities, challenges and hardships. The world has those in great supply ready to throw at us.

I have a wild idea, just bear with me.

What if we as adults become mature enough to create a world where having a different gender won't be such a terrible thing, where you won't have to be challenged to the point of suicide to be granted something you desire?

What if we don't harass children for being different?

I know. I'm a delusional optimist.

We can't be that mature, can we?

After all, we are biological machines driven by hormones preoccupied with safety, procreation and recreation.

More so, we are selfish people who want our genome to survive and don't care for anyone else's.

Worse than that, we are actively wanting for all differentness, the one we disapprove of, to just disappear from the face of the Earth so the natural order returns and we calmly sit in our cave watching the show of shadows on the wall feeling content and secure.

Everything is well with the world.

There's no climate change.

There are no conspiracy theories.

There's no reason to doubt states.

There's no hunger somewhere out there.

Just let us do our thing and don't show us disturbing images of things we cannot handle.

We want to be protected. We want our children to be protected. We don't want to think of some children out there that aren't fit to step up to the standard that is required for survival.

To that, I'll say:

Beethoven was deaf.

Da Vinci was gay.

Hawking was handicapped.

Woolf was a lesbian.

People are flawed. People are different. People aren't clean, holly, the same, perfect, etc.

People do damage to one another daily.

But the damage a state can do to people when unjust and inhumane practices become law is devastating. History teaches us as much.

If my voice counts for anything, I know in my state it doesn't because here the issue isn't even on the table, I say yes to transition as a possibility.

I say yes to early transition to those whose circumstances demand it and allow it.

I say yes to possibilities.

But I say no to the state-regulated standards for transition and medical experts making decisions in the name of their young subjects.

When a state regulates something as intimate and fluid as the gender with law, the space for mistake becomes really large.

I don't say that's the situation here and now, it's just a future I would like to avoid.

That's why I probably went there in my fiction. To see the society that would do so.

Now I just discredited myself with self-promotion and revealing my selfish motives behind everything.

I am selfish. I don't hide that. I do want to have grandchildren if that is what destiny allows.

Still, no matter our selfish motives, questions must be asked. The discussion made so that the laws when they emerge are as just as they can be.

It is a question that has to be regulated by law but it's a thin line between children's rights to childhood and systemic abuse of those who you're trying to protect.

It's a hard task to determine in what kind of an adult the young soul before us will mould itself through the experience of life.

How to distinguish between a young spiteful butch lesbian who wants to gain intimate access to females and a young fearful Trans Man who wants to gain access to male friends?

Again, I hit where it hurts.

I do that.

I hit where it hurts so you go out to treat your wound, or you get stronger where you're too soft and can be manipulated for your weakness.

How to distinguish between a young gentle gay bottom in need of care and protection trying on the drag to see will it make him more acceptable and a young Trans Woman in need of female socialization?

It's an internal distinction.

The outcome is determined in sexuality and identity as much as in gender.

Some people get satisfied with just wearing the clothes they desire.

Some people get satisfied when they completely transform into the opposite gender.

Some people stay stuck in the middle playing on the gender spectrum like it's a playground and not a serious business of breeding and succeeding in life.

The difference is often nuanced.

I know the straight cisgendered majority would like it to be simple. That they would like it for Trans People to be neatly divided into two distinct groups that support their claim how gender is an inherently binary project.

That's why Trans People who pass and did transition have the advantage of living 'normal' lives prospering in the gender they transitioned to.

That's why non-binary identities are often rejected as silly, overstated and unnecessary from the majority as much as from insiders like medically transitioned Trans People.

It's because non-binary identities and trans-identities, even if they stand under the same umbrella, stand for completely opposite ideas.

While Trans People who want to transition are a living proof that the binary gender is real, that the need to adjust to your true inner gender is the proof of how the whole gender construction is a protective shell we must strive to protect. They show us that to be in the correct gender is the matter of life and death. 'We have to transition or we'll die,' is the message here.

Non-Binary People stand for the opposite idea. Their mere existence says to us that gender is nothing serious. That the gender spectrum is just a playground you can jump on and have immense fun with. There's no reason to take it seriously here. 'We can transition even if we don't need to', is the message.

Can you see how one would agree with the cisgendered majority and the other would annoy the hell out of them?

Gender is a changing social construct that constantly adds up and loses qualities. Establishing one's identity on such a construct might lead up to feeling abandoned and angry as time goes on.

Just look at older cisgendered straight males. They are angry as hell. The sacrifices they put in the world playing faithfully their gender role just for the world to become this mad thing that says to them they should cry, be sensitive and stop being so angry.

They spit on your world deeming it worth a nice world end.

I feel better for putting my grievances out there but I'm not worried.

There are enough of us to survive as a species. Maybe my only true worry is that we might not survive because there are so many of us but we'll see how that goes in the future.

For the young Trans People, stay safe, think it through and try to see what you can suffer through and what is unacceptable because, after all, the transition itself is a challenging painful process. It is pain, persistence and it has a price to pay later on.

You can say transition is a painful medicine you receive when another way of being is more painful than the medicine itself.

Who am I to separate you from that? I would never, not consciously. I do deeply apologize if my words and call to think it thorough brought in any outcome of that nature.

Transition process is a necessary evil. A bitter medicine that cures certain kinds of incurable aches.

It's not something light young people will do out of fashion even when they go through it for other reason than dysphoria.

Anyway, I'll try to finish this off because it's a thought that is hard to finish.

Gender is the way nature lures us into sexuality.

Sexuality is the decoy that makes us submit to fertility.

When we divorce those terms, the possibilities are endless.

But I don't think there's room for worry, not too severe one.

The world will spin on, with us, or without us.

Sex vs Gender, Attraction

We discussed gender thoroughly by now.

We get it identity, vs expression, pronouns, transition, social construct and all those complicated nuanced categories.

Here we'll get on our knees to search for the basics of attraction.

What is the thing that turns us on?

That is the basic question of attraction. Attraction in return determines our model of sexual orientation.

In this modern discussion of gender, it may sometimes seem like we're reasonable beings capable of governing our passions. Like we're above our biology and can distinguish fine lines of gender to find our likings. That we're attracted to the personality more than physicality.

I'll admit, that there are individuals like that but there is the other kind of people. They see it, they like it and they want to bang it.

I say 'it' here not because I refer to all genders but because I refer to body, type of the body, and part of the body or simply someone's clothes, shoes, attire.

People are attracted to many things and more often than not it's something tangible, it's not your personality or gender, it's your physical body, your sex or your size.

That is the thing that sometimes can drive us crazy since it's unfair, primal, animalistic and outright discriminatory.

We dislike being liked for the colour of our eyes or hair.

We want to be liked for being human beings, for having a certain kind of personality, or having certain traits.

I first among you. I find it offensive when someone fixates on my body. I find it strange, uncomfortable and have nothing to give to that person because our ways of turning on mismatches.

For attraction to be ignited in anyone, there needs to be a match and the hard surface against which it ignites. That's the basic model of attraction. Something gives the spark and other thing ignites and soon there's fire all around.

(If there's fire, some of us don't burn but rather bask in the fine outline of the sunlight.)

Whatever our level of hotness is, the connection of ignition needs to be made for the fires to burn, for attraction to start and for our sexual orientation to get in motion.

Here we get to the distinction between gender and sex. To make transition and identity understandable we divided the social construct that is gender from the biological imperative that is sex.

Still, the tension continues because people are refusing to accept the distinction.

Why the resistance to such idea is so strong?

After all, it's not that hard to understand that our biology has little to do with random social signifiers of gender like length of your fingernails or length of your hair. Even less with the shape of fabric you're wearing to cover up your body while fighting cold, sun, rain and stares.

The resistance comes from the fact that the majority of people aren't attracted to gender at al_, they couldn't care less what you're wearing or how you're presenting yourself.

All they care about is what's underneath your clothes. If you have the correct set up of genitalia they are good to go.

It's quite simple because it's a sex attraction. With sex -attraction, fertility is quite important because it's a biological imperative that is created for producing babies.

Whether people admitted to it or not, we are biological beings driven by our hormones. Most of sexual intercourses, even if they aren't targeted in creating offspring, are driven on the fire of reproduction, of possibility of creation.

That's why most of adult heterosexual cisgendered adults experience this or that form of asexuality in their later years. It's because the desire for procreating was fulfilled.

That alone might be viewed as a controversial stance but it's my observation I made through conversations with people. My collected data suggests as much. It's a small sample but the pattern repeats itself so it's a worthy theory that can be studied if someone is inclined to do so.

As I studied this topic, I noticed that nowadays the world homosexual is considered offensive, as is transsexual.

The tendency is to put all words with sexuality in them as less appropriate suggests that the attraction is about gender and not sex.

I would argue that for some of us it is but there are a lot of people who would define their sexual orientation through attraction to sex regardless to gender.

Because if you put the only option to be gender-attraction most of the now straight population will have to redefine their sexuality.

By my estimation, most of the population is heterosexual and homoromantic anyway. They create sexual-reproductive connection with the opposite sex, but maintain friendship-supportive-lifetime long partnership in the same gender.

Dividing gender from sex is challenging that basic straight model in its core provoking questions they don't want to be answered.

I think that's a normal model seen in nature many times over. Females gather together to gain support and advices in raising their young while men band together to create havoc and express their natural given aggressiveness.

I know as I said it that it's probably the most backward model that exists that equates us with animals but we are slaves to our biology as much as the rest of our fellow animals are.

The majority of population is governing their lives to that basic model not giving it much thought.

When two straight people meet and discover that their genders align as their sexes are opposite, it's happy coincidence that leads to good communication in marriage, or life-time of arguments and grievances. It depends how their personalities clash.

That is the point of straightness.

It's less important how your personalities clash as long as your sexes clashed in a way that produced a new generation of humans. Mission accomplished, now let's live together to the best of our possibilities.

The notion of gender-attraction is a noble one, a fine way to move forward and claim our minds can triumph over our biology.

The truth is that no matter how gender expression changes, and you might notice how it changes drastically over the time-frame of a few centuries, the basic sex-attraction remains the same.

Still, as we move away from the basic model that is most widely spread, we can see sexuality, identity and gender making variants that are different than those strictly biologically driven.

When we divorce sexuality from fertility, sex from gender, other types of factors come into play when it comes to attraction and people start to react to different types of triggers that ignite their inner fires.

As we play with our gender and explore our sexuality, it might be polite of us to notice and acknowledge people who are different than us, that are attracted differently than us, whose sexuality is bound to sex and fertility.

For them, we can be generous and leave the terms like homosexuality, heterosexuality and bisexuality in. They are simple signifiers that you have sex preference rather than a gender one as we move forward to see which terms will survive the test of time and which will be forgotten in the tides of tomorrows.

Sexualisation and Demonization

Morality and sexuality are eternally entwined no matter how we tried to push the religion out of our bed.

Sexuality is the fastest way to be pushed to hell of any religion. To control sexuality is to control your subjects making them behave, do their chores and not descend into madness of promiscuity and orgies.

That is the ultimate fear any complex society can have, the descent into immoral behaviour, over-indulging and abandoning your duties for pleasure.

Sometimes there can be a sense that the Roman Empire fell apart because of their upper echelons over-indulgence and decadency. But that, of course, can just be a moralistic view of the Christianity that replaced them. Reasons were probably more political and war induced than anything else but the sense of morality is what we are left with.

Christianity brought in the firm sense of morality and rules for any form of sexuality. That is for the western part of the history. It was different on other places but Islam wasn't any kinder towards sexual differences.

Sexuality was demonized, it was the demonic force in you that made you do things that are hellish, desire things that are forbidden.

These days, even if we still live in society that is ruled by Christian values, sexualisation has a stronger impact than demonization even if it leads to god-fearing people to see anything sexual as demonic in its nature.

To be queer is to stare off with that accusation of being a demon and reclaiming your identity as valid and morally just.

That is the end goal of any affirmation, to be acknowledged as morally just.

Many may contradict this claim and resist its implications but as we move from obscure corners and hidden alleys moving towards legalization, protection and social acceptance we move towards morality.

More than any law, morality is what makes socially acceptable behaviour. It's what makes socially acceptable individuals.

To be socially acceptable sexuality has to be trimmed to determine what is morally acceptable and what will still be considered to be a sin.

The modern-day gays are less fiercely targeted at their goal of sexual satisfaction at any cost because their sexuality is in the public eye, it will be discussed as much as the immoral sexuality of any political leader of famous actor.

Marriage equality brings in rights but also obligations. It's implied that marriage demands fidelity and infidelity will be punished no matter is it gay or straight infidelity and that is equality in a nutshell.

The punishment and moral control will now be distributed equally to all parties no matter their gender, identity or sexual orientation.

What was before coding, signalling, secret passwords to convey identity and finding a hook-up, now is a language that is in the process of integration in the main language. All these terms that were fought for so fiercely, will now be understand by the broader community and when they hear them they will know what they mean.

The seclusion of a secret identity will come to an end.

For some of us.

Those who are still on the other side of the law secluded by desires and drives that aren't in the public eye or accepted will still have their secret codes for recognizing each other.

I don't feel like I'm exposing anyone with this dictionary since I only used terms that are easily accessible online and anyone interested can find and understand them.

After all, this is what the fight was all about. To be integrated, to be accepted, to be recognized as valid members of the society, to be stopped called derogatory names, to be valued.

Still, as we cross this threshold into the visibility I advise caution because in this world morality that is unwritten in the law is often more valuable than legality.

On this side, women who were overly sexual were called Jezebels. It was a way to make an equation between a sexual woman and a woman who killed righteous warriors.

Sexualisation is in full throttle, everything is thrown out the media machine looking sexually appealing but on the street people are still looking to see who breaks moral codes and who abides by them.

I'm probably overly cautious but history is treacherous. You seem to be winning in one moment but in another tides turn. Morality is our inner sense of what is right and what is wrong. It might feel strange to bring that up here in the midst of discussion of all things that can be queer but queerness isn't equated with immorality anymore, it's not a subversive element living in abandoned buildings thrown out of their homes.

Some of us still do live like that but for people who still live like that it would be nice to bring some order to chaos and make it a lesser of an occurrence.

To be queer isn't to be demonic.

To be queer isn't to be immoral.

To be queer isn't to be an outcast.

It doesn't have to be anymore.

To be queer is to be brave.

To be queer is to be different.

To be queer is to face off with your own demonic reflexion and emerge loving the humanity of it.

To be queer is to take a slur, turn it inside out, and to wear it like the most exquisite accessory you can find.

To be queer is to be victorious.

Because there is a great sense of victory in facing off with a demand to stay quiet, to stay closeted, to stay hidden under a threat of being beaten, raped, mistreated, insulted, stepped on, murdered and humiliated. Being faced with all that and choosing bravery, choosing loudness, choosing flashiness, choosing a life of honesty rather than a life of falseness is a victory in itself.

That's why I think there is a great sense of morality in being queer.

Because that's one of our main cultural values we as humans share, being truthful, choosing truth when a lie would keep you safe. Not accepting the label of demonic but instead lifting up a heavy mirror for the general public to see their own demonic reflexion.

Being honest and authentic when all that brings you is pain.

That is the definition of moral strength and value.

Conclusion:

Aka, something that will make an ending. A way for us to pretend how anything ever truly ends.

Not Everything we Try will Survive

Questioning and experimentation are a natural part of any process of examination of the world. It's the way most sciences operate to understand the world we live in.

It's natural that not all theories are true. Most of them get disproven this way or another.

It's easy with theories that can be disproven. Those that can't are trickier.

It's easier to find what is false than what is true.

When something is false, you find a proof that disproves the theory. When you can't find fault in something, it's always an option that some proof will be noticed down the line.

Truth is elusive and all encompassing. What is, envelops us like air. We can barely notice that air exists. Its existence wasn't easy to prove, to weigh the air we breathe.

As the water is invisible to the fish, most of truths are hard to notice for us, they can be observed only through their faults, when something falls out of alignment. Like gravity was discovered when an apple fell on a head instead to the ground.

When gravity was discovered, laws it forces us to abide by didn't change. We now only had an understanding of the force that holds us glued to the ground on a spinning ball that is our Earth.

Sexuality, fertility and sex won't change by our exploration of the same. Gender might change since it's not embedded in our genome but rather constructed by our minds but gender changes regardless of our poking at its contents.

Some of us will change our sex, some of us will lose our fertility giving it away as a price for a happy free existence where we don't have to strain ourselves to fit a box we're not cut out to fit in.

Some of us will play crossing borders and retreating back behind them trying to see what fits our unfathomable form.

Some of us won't play at all holding on to our right to restrain ourselves from participating in a game we have no desire for, see no purpose of or find no pleasure in.

Some of us will grow old to be bitter of our choices, to be angry on the world that changed the rules again just when we managed to abide by them but that's ok, that happens to people who don't play with gender, sexuality and sex at all too.

Some of us will grow old to be bitter at the world that didn't change quick enough, that turned in the wrong direction, angry on young generation for being silly and irresponsible when you fought so hard for their rights.

Different destinies will hit us differently because we're not a monolith with the one and the same life-experience, with the same experiment we're conducting. More likely, we're dancing our own dances on a shared stage trying to convince the world that our act is the one it should be included in the official assembly before the general audiences.

Not all of us will make the cut but the stage for rehearsals should always stay there for new dancers to offer new choreographies they think life should consist of.

Even when refused by the managing director of life, our dances continue on the private stage of life because we are directors of our private arena.

No matter what shape our society takes on there should always be at least three stages included in it.

The General Stage, where performers show us what approved and current life is all about.

The Rehearsal Stage, where small groups can present their ideas of how approved life should be adjusted next to improve upon the stage we're all staring at.

The Private Arena, where we can make choreographies of our own because privacy is the place sexuality, intimacy, fertility and sex take place, were we can perform our gender with less fervency, where we get to decide which parts of the general dance we'll perform for ourselves.

Sometimes, that's what makes life satisfying, not just staring at the general stage and mimicking what we see to the smallest move but to feel we are the dancers creating our own unique dance that can't be replicated by anyone else. A dance that will perish with us but the beauty of the dance isn't in its endurance, it's a movement that disappears as soon as it's made. It's a breath-taking act of living each moment. Who's there to witness it can have it in the eye of their memory, who doesn't show up for the show will never even know it happened.

Not every dance we make will survive to be repeated by others but the mere act of creating it might be the thing that makes your life worth your while.

I Don't Have to Like you, but I Have to Respect you

You can't force anyone to like someone because liking is an internal process of producing positive hormones when seeing someone. It can't be faked.

But you can force people to respect others because respect is an outer way we treat others. It can be faked.

I don't care if your respect is fake, I'll take it.

That is basically what we demand, like Aretha nicely put it, respect.

That is the place I feel we should draw the line in the sand because when you cross it you break other people's boundaries. No one owes you their feelings, no one owes you their intimacy and no one owes you liking.

Liking, loving and especially attraction are very discriminatory processes, there's nothing democratic about them. Usually, we like a really small percentage of people.

To apply models like racism to sexuality is to start a witch hunt. Of course, you can prefer a race, you can prefer eyes, you can prefer a type of hands, a type of nails, laughter, hair, hairstyle, attraction is discriminatory as something can get.

We're most likely attracted to people who share some characteristics with people who nurtured us when we were babies. Much like a stork who fixates on a lamp if she sees a lamp as soon as she hatches, we humans are also deeply programmed about what attracts, moves and endears us.

Sexuality can divorce fertility and it does both in human and animal kingdoms, but we can't divorce our small brain that tells us who we dig and who doesn't do anything for us.

For that sake, just try to put away pitches and forks when someone tells you their preference. Think about it, why you would want to be granted an opportunity with someone who wouldn't prefer you over all others.

But maybe I'm just a romantic at heart thinking how love is in store for all of us. It isn't. Some of us aren't buying love at all and that's ok.

Still, the next time when some hot white dude tells how he prefers other hot white dudes before getting offended pause to think of your own internalized racism. Why should we care what hot white dudes like or dislike?

Are we like that proverbial stork? Did we stare at the screen full of white dudes for so long that we fixated on something that couldn't love us back for the life of it?

Anonymity as Protection

Living out in the open is the epitome of a fulfilled queer life lived in all colours of the rainbow of joy.

Not living out in the open is called staying in the closet, going under radar and stealth implying there is something limiting, bad and almost immoral in going in incognito mode through life.

We should all stand tall and proud so the world can see us, hear us and get used to us.

For myself, I always say how I never was in the closet to begin with.

At first, I had no idea there was something I should be closed in the closet for. Later, I just stated what I am in normal terms without labels but without labels, people would just normalize what I said to them. Like, 'yeah, I'm a man too, I know what you mean.'

Walking through life not offering people labels but explanations I gained a feeling that straight people might not be as straight as the label advertised it to be.

But that's the way with labels, they are inevitably a simplification of the complex insides of the bottle.

When I started to use labels to shorten the explanation, the reaction was starkly different. An offended kind of shock appeared like I cheated when I explained things simply.

Saying to people I'm more a man than a woman, I'm manly like that, I have a personality of a man, I'm a man within, doesn't have the same ring to it as I'm a Trans Man, although the content is the same.

Labels mark us and give us an easy way to pronounce our identity but they also serve as dividers between us and them.

That's how it is with any discriminatory distinction. Anything that makes a difference creates a border and that's ok. That's why we have borders between countries, to establish the difference between identities.

You and I aren't one and the same.

That shouldn't be an inflammatory sentence that causes war that lasts for centuries.

Yet, sometimes it does. It makes life much harder and challenging. Sometimes even life-threatening.

On the other hand, anonymity is a protection of sorts, when people don't know you're different, they forget to treat you differently.

Don't feel ashamed when you use the comfort of that protection. You owe no one your identity, your sexuality or your body. They are yours to protect and dispose of.

As I'm putting down the protection of my anonymity as a worn-out old skin, I wish you luck in your endeavours. Stay safe, be wise and remember that the truth of your heart you owe only to yourself.

The Exit, the Place Where we Stop

We have to stop somewhere with everything in life. There is a place where we have to abruptly leave everything as it is and put time into something else that demands our attention.

This dictionary is by no means complete. There are many more terms that aren't included and many more terms that will be created as we move towards the future.

My dictionary is an attempt to capture a cultural moment frozen in time. As time progresses forward we'll see in which direction our society will turn because societies are like humans. Everything seems the same old same old until it abruptly drops what it was doing and starts to do something completely new.

As a time traveller travelling forward in time, what we all are, I experienced first-hand a few of those turns when things change from today to tomorrow too drastically to completely comprehend.

But never mind, the change is life. The change is even death when things go into decay and entropy starts to multiply until something new is born out of the chaos.

I'll now shut this door behind me leaving these ruins to be examined by some future historian while

I'm off to create some more havoc that will convey
meaning I'm still not aware of.

Finishing notes:

Aka, justifications. Blame these other people for misinformation. Just kidding, any project of cultural phenomena is like a play of echoes because the culture itself is created in echoes of words that we give each other. We don't stand alone but in the context of the greater societal structure. To assure you I didn't just made up all the words used above I'll list below some people whose echoes I put between my lines to give me context and credibility.

Context Lenses

Some YouTubers, comedians and reporters I owe gratitude to for explaining the context of some queer, and world, issues I had no knowledge of. They are kind enough and brave enough to expose their journeys and lives so others can see their example and find solace in their struggles and wisdom. Views exposed in this book are my own so don't go to their door with torches, only with kind words, please, respect is what we owe each other.

Still, listening to them and thinking of their words did bring me the understanding that stands behind this book so you might say they inspired me to do more.

AreTheyGay

Ash Hardell

ContraPoints

Council of Geeks

Philosophy Tube

Jammidodger

Jessie Gender

Kat Blaque

Linsday Ellis

John Oliver

Some More News

Todrick Hall
Trevor Noah
Ty Turner

Here I listed a few of prominent queer voices I listened through the years, and some who aren't on the queer side of identity but have insights in the general society that are helpful in creating in a more comprehensive picture of the current state of affairs in our society that is Earth.

Of course, I listened other voices too, conservative as subversive but I won't list them here since their credentials for speaking on behalf of Queer Culture are somewhat dubious.

For me, you'll find my queer credentials when you turn the page. My official credentials are in there too, my diploma of Philosophy and Sociology but I also put my origin since I think of that as a defining factor that might be colouring my perspective removing my perspective from the mainstream view.

I tried to be as objective as I can in this small dictionary that I composed to expose my own opinions and bias. Still, the ultimate objectivity is an ideal that can't be obtained because we all are bound to our individual lens through which we observe the world.

My lenses are as follows:

My bias, if you're unable to read it out from the text of my credentials, is that I was born and raised in a country with history of communism and fascism, with family members that were on the wrong side of history. That's why I will always be on the lookout for the signs of any structure turning totalitarian on us.

I'm, of course, biased since I'm queer. That makes my views removed to the left.

On the other side, I'm biased since I'm Croatian so my perspective on the world is starting from the land that is strictly conservative, deeply religious and preoccupied with morals. That will skew my moral compass to the right.

Since I'm socialized as a woman I will understand female struggle better so I'll slide towards female rights.

But in the basic level male perspective is much easier to see for me.

In relation to diversity, colour, race and other polarizing topics I will have to rely on foreign experts and my ability to intellectually discern different topics since my country is predominantly white and Catholic so my experience on those matters are as limited as they can be.

The fact that I have a religious upbringing, Catholic religious upbringing, means that my stances won't be what you expect of them to be in the matters of morality but I do try to keep an open mind.

Although I did my best to socialize as a woman, my perspective on femininity will always be that of an outsider since I never managed to crack the essence of femininity always staying silly in my attempt to perform femininity. I will probably suffer from the same limitations my male colleagues suffer from too.

For the Queer Culture, I'm an outsider here too since I had no participation in any form of the Queer Culture, not even the limited kind Croatia can offer.

I guess I'm an outsider everywhere since I never was socialized as a man but that maybe makes my perspective skewed enough to bring something new to the table.

Whatever that may be, I'm offering it to you with sincerity even if it may lack objectivity of a scientist who is truly detached or insight of the insider who experienced queer perspective in its fullest.

With that, I bid you farewell taking out my passport to exit through the travelling portal to embark on a new adventure.

My Queer Passport

(Or, my credentials for allowing myself to write this dictionary)

Name:	Riva Zmajoki
Birth Year:	1982
Country of Origin:	Croatia, Europe (A part of the Communistic Republic of Yugoslavia at the time of my birth. Nowadays a part of the European Union.)
Gender:	Transgender, Medically Transitioned from Intersex to Female without consent. Upon birth received Sex Changing surgery. In my teens received hormones to finish my transition without my awareness of the process.
Gender Identity:	Male
Gender Expression:	Fluid, it changes with the seasons and often every few years from very feminine, over neutral non-binary, to masculine and back. (It's been like that since childhood. I've been doing it without understanding what the process was about.)
Social Gender:	Gender Conforming to Female. I have no intention of undergoing medical procedures of altering my sex or disputing the official gender in my official papers. I accept being addressed as a woman and the identity that is expected of me to perform. (It's another thing how

	poorly I perform my assigned gender.)
Sex:	MAAB, Intersex
Sexual Orientation:	Asexual, Demisexual, Sapiosexual, Bisexual with preference for men.
Romantic Inclination:	Panromantic
Given name:	Iva Šakić (A nickname and a way to remind old people who I am. Not offended when used.)
Married Name:	Iva Šakić Ristić (Dead name)
Pronoun:	She/Her (although I won't take offence if you get it wrong, recently I wore a flowered dress and entered a hardware store where I was addressed as a Mr even if in Croatia being Transgender isn't even a thing people were aware of. Did not take offence, just proceeded with my purchase.)
Questioning phase:	I knew I was bisexual from very early on. Understanding that I'm asexual came in my mid-thirties. That was the time I started to explore my gender considering am I a Trans Man. Only at the end of my thirties did I realize my Intersex physique and the nature of my transition. That brought me to understand my fluid expression and personality better.
Occupation:	A Writer, A Poet, A Philosopher, A YouTuber, A Publisher
Degree:	Philosophy and Sociology, Master of Science

Sources of Terms

acronyms.thefreedictionary.com

aifs.gov.au

americanaddictioncenters.org

amherst.edu

aminoapps.com

amnesty.org

aromantic.wikia.org

asexuality.org

asexualitytrust.org.nz

bbc.com

britannica.com

cbrc.net

cosmopolitan.com

culturalbridgestojustice.org

dailydot.com

dictionary.cambrige.org

dictionary.com

economist.com

eu.usatoday.com

gender.wikia.org

glamour.com

google.com

health4men.co.za

healthline.com

hrc.org

insider.com

languages.oup.com

lgbt.ucsf.edu

lgbta.wikia.org

lgbtq.multicultural.ufl.edu

lgbtq.smcgov.org

lgbtqia.ucdavis.edu

lgbtqiahealtheducation.org

link.springer.com

math.iup.edu

medicalnewstoday.com

medicinenet.com

meritocracy.is

merriam-webster.com

mindbodygreen.com

mogaipedia.org

ncbi.nlm.nih.gov

newyorker.com

nonbinary.wiki

nytimes.com

outrightinternational.org

oxfordlearnersdictionaries.com

pflag.org

plannedparenthood.org

press.princteon.edu

queerdom.fandom.com

quora.com

quotev.com

sparknotes.com

stonewall.org.uk

theatlantic.com

theconversation.com

theguardian.com

thereckoningmag.com

thesafezoneproject.com

time.com

timesofindia.indiatimes.com

translate.google.com

unaids.org

urbandictionary.com

verywellhelth.com

vox.com

wearefamilycharleston.org

wikia.org

wikipedia.com

wired.com

wearefamilycharleston.org

webmd.com

yourdictionary.com

Etc…

Index